LET'S STUDY
JAMES

In the same series:

LET'S STUDY MATTHEW by Mark E. Ross
LET'S STUDY MARK by Sinclair B. Ferguson
LET'S STUDY LUKE by Douglas J. W. Milne
LET'S STUDY JOHN by Mark G. Johnston
LET'S STUDY ACTS by Dennis E. Johnson
LET'S STUDY 1 CORINTHIANS by David Jackman
LET'S STUDY 2 CORINTHIANS by Derek Prime
LET'S STUDY GALATIANS by Derek Thomas
LET'S STUDY EPHESIANS by Sinclair B. Ferguson
LET'S STUDY PHILIPPIANS by Sinclair B. Ferguson
LET'S STUDY COLOSSIANS & PHILEMON by Mark G. Johnston
LET'S STUDY 1 & 2 THESSALONIANS by Andrew W. Young
LET'S STUDY 1 TIMOTHY by W. John Cook
LET'S STUDY HEBREWS by Hywel R. Jones
LET'S STUDY 1 PETER by William W. Harrell
LET'S STUDY 2 PETER & JUDE by Mark G. Johnston
LET'S STUDY THE LETTERS OF JOHN by Ian Hamilton
LET'S STUDY REVELATION by Derek Thomas

Series Editor: SINCLAIR B. FERGUSON

Let's Study
JAMES

Sinclair B. Ferguson

THE BANNER OF TRUTH TRUST

THE BANNER OF TRUTH TRUST
3 Murrayfield Road, Edinburgh EH12 6EL, UK
P.O. Box 621, Carlisle, PA 17013, USA

*

First published 2018
© Sinclair B. Ferguson 2018
Reprinted 2020

ISBN

Print: 978 1 84871 846 3
EPUB: 978 1 84871 847 0
Kindle: 978 1 84871 848 7

*

*

Typeset in 11/12.5 pt Ehrhardt MT at
The Banner of Truth Trust,
Edinburgh

Printed in the USA by
Versa Press, Inc.,
East Peoria, IL

To
Derek and Rosemary Thomas
In affection and gratitude
Psalm 133:1-3

Contents

PUBLISHER'S PREFACE   ix

OUTLINE OF JAMES   xi

INTRODUCTION   xiii

1.   Experiencing Faith's Trials (1:1-4)   1
2.   Asking for Wisdom (1:5-11)   9
3.   Understanding Temptation (1:12-18)   19
4.   Obeying God's Word (1:19-27)   31
5.   Impartiality in the Church (2:1-13)   41
6.   Faith That Works (2:14-26)   51
7.   Guarding the Tongue (3:1-12)   61
8.   Showing Heavenly Wisdom (3:13-18)   69
9.   Avoiding Worldliness (4:1-6)   81
10.   Expressing Repentance (4:7-12)   89
11.   The Unpredictability of Life (4:13-17)   97
12.   The Danger of False Riches (5:1-6)   103
13.   Patience Until Christ Returns (5:7-12)   111
14.   The Needs of God's People (5:13-20)   119

GROUP STUDY GUIDE   129

FOR FURTHER READING   141

Publisher's Preface

*L*et's *Study James* is part of a series of books which seek to explain and apply the message of Scripture. The series is designed to meet a specific and important need in the church. While not technical commentaries, the volumes comment on the text of a biblical book; and, without being merely lists of practical applications, they are concerned with the ways in which the teaching of Scripture can affect and transform our lives today. Understanding the Bible's message and applying its teaching are the aims.

Like other volumes in the series, *Let's Study James* seeks to combine explanation and application. Its concern is to be helpful to ordinary Christian people by encouraging them to understand the message of the Bible and apply it to their own lives. The reader in view is not the person who is interested in all the detailed questions which fascinate the scholar, although behind the writing of each study lies an appreciation for careful and detailed scholarship. The aim is exposition of Scripture written in the language of a friend, seated alongside you with an open Bible.

Let's Study James is designed to be used in various contexts. It can be used simply as an aid for individual Bible study. Some may find it helpful to use in their devotions with husband or wife, or to read in the context of the whole family.

In order to make these studies more useful, not only for individual use but also for group study in Sunday School classes and home, church or college, study guide material will be found on pp. 129-140. Sometimes we come away frustrated rather than helped by group discussions. Frequently that is because we have been encouraged to discuss a passage of Scripture which we do not understand very well in the first place. Understanding must always be the foundation for enriching discussion and for thoughtful, practical application. Thus, in addition to the exposition of James, the additional material provides questions to encourage personal thought and study, or to be used as discussion starters. The Group Study Guide divides the material into thirteen sections and provides direction for leading and participating in group study and discussion.

Outline of James

I. 1:1-27: THE BASICS OF FAITH
    (i) 1:1-4: Experiencing Various Trials
    (ii) 1:5-11: Asking for Wisdom
    (iii) 1:12-18: Understanding Temptation
    (iv) 1:19-27: Obeying God's Word

II. 2:1-26: HOW FAITH WORKS
    (i) 2:1-13: Impartiality in the Church
    (ii) 2:14-26: Faith That Works

III. 3:1–4:12: MARKS OF CONSISTENT FAITH
    (i) 3:1-12: Guarding the Tongue
    (ii) 3:13-18: Showing Heavenly Wisdom
    (iii) 4:1-6: Avoiding Worldliness
    (iv) 4:7-12: Expressing Repentance

IV. 4:13–5:20: LIVING BY FAITH NOT BY SIGHT
    (i) 4:13-17: The Unpredictability of Life
    (ii) 5:1-6: The Danger of False Riches
    (iii) 5:7-12: Patience until Christ Returns
    (iv) 5:13-20: The Needs of God's People

Introduction

'James, a servant of God and of the Lord Jesus Christ, To the twelve tribes in the Dispersion: Greetings' (James 1:1). With these words 'James' introduces his short letter. Throughout the centuries it has proved to be an excellent refresher course in what it means to live the Christian life. It is only a few pages long. It can be read out loud in twenty minutes. It is very direct and extremely practical.

If you were a Christian publisher today it would be easy to give it a catchy title; perhaps something like *Getting Your Faith in Working Order* or *Faith Works Hard*. But notice the word 'faith'. For while many Christians think of this letter in terms of the practical counsel it gives about what we are to do, it is really about faith, or, borrowing an expression from the apostle Paul, about 'faith working through love' (Gal. 5:6). Perhaps James had preached a short series of sermons on this theme and was now sharing the teaching he had given with a wider group of first-century Christians by means of this letter.

What do you do on those (increasingly rare) occasions when you receive a letter? First of all, you want to know who wrote it. And then you want to know why they have written and what they want to say to you.

I. JAMES WHO?

For most of us the question, 'Who?' makes a great deal of difference to the way we read a letter. If we do not recognize the handwriting, we turn to the end of the letter to find the signature. What if the signature is 'James'? No problem? Unless you have several friends named 'James'. Then, of course, since your correspondent probably knows that, he will sign his name 'James (Smith)', or 'James (Jones)'.

If someone in the family asks, 'Who is your letter from?' and you reply 'James', you may receive the slightly irritated response, 'Yes, but James who …?' If you then respond with the surname, the reply is likely to be, 'Oh, *that* James.'

But in the case of this New Testament letter, exactly who is 'that James'? He describes himself only as 'James, a servant of God and of the Lord Jesus Christ' (1:1). But the New Testament mentions several men called 'James'. Which—if any of them—is our author?

Does he give us any clues that would help us to establish his identity?

Clearly 'James' was someone who knew that when he introduced himself his identity would be well enough known for his letter to be welcomed appreciatively and read carefully.

He was someone who knew the Palestinian world well. In James 5:7 he refers to the distinctive early and late rains. Both he and his readers were familiar with the idea of the Diaspora, or Dispersion— the people of Israel who had been scattered throughout the nations following the exile—because he describes his (Christian) recipients as 'the twelve tribes in the Dispersion' (1:1). He calls Abraham 'our father' (2:21); he assumes his readers and hearers are familiar with his story as well as those of Rahab (2:25), the prophets (5:10), Job (5:11) and Elijah (5:17). In all likelihood, therefore, it looks as if most of the recipients of his letter were Jewish Christians who had been 'exiled' because of the persecution of the early church (See Acts 8:1; 11:19).

Of the men we know in the early church called 'James', there are only two who could have written this letter with the sense of authority it carries, and the assumption that its readers and hearers would receive it well.

One is James the apostle, the brother of John. He was executed by Herod in 44 A.D. (Acts 12:2). There is, however, no hint in the letter that it comes from an apostle. James introduces himself only as 'a servant' (1:1). Almost certainly he is the brother of Jude who specifically introduces himself as 'brother of James' (Jude verse 1), and therefore none other than James the son of Joseph. Whether he was the son of Joseph and Mary, or the child of an earlier marriage of Joseph, in either case he was the half-brother of Jesus.

Introduction

What do we know about James?

- James must have lived for many years in the same family as Jesus. He was probably named after Joseph's father Jacob (Matt. 1:16).
- We know that earlier in Jesus' ministry he was not a believer. John tells us that 'not even his brothers believed in him' (John 7:5). At some point, however, he became a believer. Following the resurrection, Jesus specifically appeared to him (1 Cor. 15:7). He was present with his other brothers in the Upper Room as they waited for the Day of Pentecost (Acts 1:14).
- In due course, he seems to have become the leading figure in the Jerusalem church. When Simon Peter was set free from prison by the intervention of an angel, he insisted that those who first learned the news at the house of John Mark's mother should 'tell these things to James and to the brothers' (Acts 12:17)—almost certainly an indication of the position of leadership in which James now stood. Later at the 'Council of Jerusalem' when the apostles gathered with the elders to discuss the implications of the conversion of Gentiles, James seems to have served as the spokesman for the Jerusalem (Jewish) church, and indeed as the moderator of the gathering (Acts 15:13, 19). His leadership is further confirmed by Paul's visit to him recorded in Acts 21:18, and by the references to him in Galatians 1:19 and 2:9, 12.
- There are striking resemblances between the speech James made at the 'Council of Jerusalem' and passages in this letter (with James 1:1 compare Acts 15:23; with James 2:5 compare Acts 15:13; with James 2:7 compare Acts 15:17).

It is not surprising therefore that most students of the New Testament have identified the author of this letter as James the half-brother of Jesus. If he was—and we will assume this to be the case—what a privilege it is to have access to the teaching of someone who had lived in Jesus' family, and who spoke of him so lovingly as the Lord Jesus Christ (1:1), and as 'the Lord of glory' (2:1).

II. THE FIRST RECIPIENTS

James describes his audience as 'the twelve tribes in the Dispersion' (1:1). They are the believers of the new diaspora of which Simon Peter would also write (1 Pet. 1:1). They are therefore largely believers with a Jewish background. They meet as a Christian synagogue (*sunagogē*, 2:2). They seem to have come from various social and economic backgrounds, some more, others less prosperous (1:10; 4:13-17). In all likelihood most of them had suffered significant privation and had perhaps been impoverished by disinheritance. They were now exiles facing severe hardships. They had been taken to court by the rich (2:7); their faith had been mocked; others had taken advantage of them in their weakness (5:4-6). The Christian life is tough enough; but it must have been doubly difficult to be a Christian cut off from the old social network of support and to face the ravages of persecution, emigration and subsequent poverty.

III. WHY WRITE?

James does not tell us explicitly why he wrote—unlike the apostle John, for example, who wrote his First Letter to encourage assurance (1 John 5:13). But several themes run through the Letter of James and make clear what his burden is. He writes about suffering and joy, riches and poverty, faith and works, the tongue and speech, and about wisdom and folly. In a word he writes about the heart and life of the Christian believer.

Undergirding all this there appears to be a central pastoral concern: he wants to see his Christian friends growing into well-rounded and mature Christians (1:4), believers whose faith is in good working order, who have learned to be patient and steadfast in the face of suffering and persecution, and who function well in the fellowship of the church. He discusses the varied characteristics of the mature Christian, the responsibilities of new life in Christ, and the means by which God enables us to grow. He is concerned that Christian disciples should be marked by a heavenly wisdom.

The Letter of James thus covers a wide variety of topics. It has a challenging and practical focus. It expresses a concern for rigorously consistent God-honouring living. James's *bête noire* is false and hollow piety; pious platitudes are anathema to him. Faith that does not issue in good works, a holy life, concern for the needy, and a disciplined use of the tongue, is for James no faith at all. On such themes as these he writes with passion and energy, the index of which is that in the course of the five chapters of his letter we will encounter one imperative (command) for approximately every two verses he writes.

To the content of his letter we can now turn.

I

Experiencing Faith's Trials

James, a servant of God and of the Lord Jesus Christ, To the twelve tribes in the Dispersion: Greetings. ² Count it all joy, my brothers, when you meet trials of various kinds, ³ for you know that the testing of your faith produces steadfastness. ⁴ And let steadfastness have its full effect, that you may be perfect and complete, lacking in nothing.

(James 1:1-4)

James, as we have seen, was almost certainly the half-brother of the Lord Jesus, and had lived with him in what we would regard as a large family. There seem to have been at least eight children: Jesus himself, plus James, Joseph, Simon and Judas (Jude), as well as at least three sisters (Matt. 13:55-56 refers to 'all his sisters' which must, presumably, mean he had more than two). But the New Testament sheds little light on what family life was like for Jesus. On occasions we find little hints, but no more than suggestions, possible implications drawn from the way in which Jesus talked about family life. James was probably the eldest of the other brothers (Matt. 13:55 lists him first). To some readers he can appear somewhat austere, strict, even sharp. But by the time we have finished reading his whole letter and reflected on his words it is hard not to admire him and to feel an affection for him. He has a pastor's heart. For him 'out of sight' is by no means 'out of mind' and so he is writing to his Christian friends to give them encouragement and guidance.

James introduces himself, however, not as 'the brother of Jesus', but as 'a servant of God and of the Lord Jesus Christ'.

There is a radical significance to the choice of 'servant'. It means *slave*. To be a slave meant that one's life was owned by another. James regarded himself in this relation to Jesus! In describing himself thus he is encouraging his readers to think of themselves in the same way. For to be such a servant means saying of Christ: 'What he says to me, I will do; what he asks of me, I will give; where he sends me, I will go.' That was not always so for James. Indeed, he surely must have experienced an extended struggle before he was brought to yield to the Saviour. Earlier in Jesus' ministry he and his brothers had not 'believed' (John 7:5). But now anything less than absolute commitment by himself was intolerable, and he regarded anything inferior in another as inconsistent. New Testament Christians are like those Old Testament slaves who said, 'I love my master, … I will not go out free' (Exod. 21:5-6).

But on the other hand, the phrase 'servant of God' has its roots in the pages of the Old Testament. It was the way God described Moses ('my servant Moses', Num. 12:7), and the way the young Samuel had been taught to speak to the Lord ('Speak, LORD, for your servant hears', 1 Sam. 3:9). Most of all it was the title given to the one who would come to be the suffering Servant and the Saviour of his people (Isa. 42:1; 49:3; 50:10; 52:13–53:12). It is a title not only of absolute commitment but also of great honour.

Coupled with this, however, James describes himself as 'a servant of God and of the Lord Jesus Christ'. It would be easy to read on without noting the enormous significance of such a statement. But we should pause and feel the weight of this description. For here James couples the name of Jesus with God. He describes his own relationship with them (servant) as identical.

This is one of many indications that the New Testament's teaching about the deity of Jesus is not confined to a small number of 'proof texts'. It is all-pervasive. Here, in a context in which we might assume the writer penned his words instinctively rather than with slow and measured care, we find him expressing his deepest conviction about the identity of Jesus. He is 'the Lord'. The very fact that James—clearly a deeply religious monotheistic Jew—could so easily and naturally (one might even say casually) refer to God and Christ in the same breath underscores the depth of his conviction that Jesus was not only the son of Mary but the Son of God.

Not only so, but James calls Jesus 'Lord', that is *Kurios*, the stand-ard Greek translation of Yahweh, the special covenant name of God in the Hebrew Bible. In the Jewish world in which James had been nurtured this was an audacious claim and open to the charge of blasphemy. In the Roman world (where Caesar was the divine 'Lord') it was a dangerous claim and open to the charge of treason. But James is in no doubt about Jesus' identity. He is the glorious 'Lord Jesus' (2:1).

We do not know exactly when James came to believe in Christ in this way. His story teaches us a simple but vital lesson. Not even the very best of family relations provides us with entrance into the kingdom of God. In that sense, even for a relative of Jesus, the flesh profits nothing (John 6:63).

Notice what flows from this remarkable testimony to his half-brother with whom he spent years in the same family home. For his description of himself flows from his understanding of Jesus' identity. He is Lord, James is his servant. When faith was born in him, he saw the glory of his Saviour, and his heart was subdued to love and serve him.

Not only James, but all Christians are servants, bond slaves, of Jesus (Rom. 6:17). Yes, we are more (we are 'friends', John 15:14-15; we are 'brothers' and 'children', Heb. 2:11, 13-14); but we are never less. Our lives, our wills, our destinies are all his. We are called to make his will our will, his pleasure our pleasure, his glory our goal.

But if James describes himself first as a servant in relationship to Jesus, rather than his relative, he thinks of his correspondents as 'my brothers' (1:2). By grace, through faith, they have all become members of the family of Jesus! He addresses them as 'the twelve tribes in the Dispersion' (1:1). We are given no further information about the specific identity of these Christians. The fact that he describes them as 'the twelve tribes' may reflect both their Jewish background and the fact that they are the true children of Abraham. They have been drawn to Christ by grace; they have now been dispersed into the world with the gospel.

James sends them 'Greetings'. As his letter makes clear, his basic concern for them is that they will grow to maturity.

What will follow these opening 'Greetings' (1:1)? What will James say? What would you say are the most important principles to grasp in order to become a fully mature Christian? James's answer might come as a surprise to members of the church in the twenty-first century.

[3]

VARIOUS TRIALS

James comes straight to the point. His opening words may indeed surprise us. Yet they are very similar to the opening words of the other New Testament letter written to the Dispersion (1:1, cf. 1 Pet. 1:1). James is writing to Christians undergoing 'trials of various kinds'. What are they to do? How should they react?

Our tendency when we face trials is probably either to shrivel up in defeat and become passive, perhaps even self-pitying; or, on the other hand, to clench our teeth and fists and to rely on our own strength to battle on against the odds. But for James either of these reactions would appear desperately short-sighted and lacking in any real appreciation of the teaching of Jesus. For James trials are the inevitable experience of those who live, on the one hand, in the light of Christ's coming and their new birth (1:18) but, on the other, prior to the return of Christ (2:5). Living between these two points in history means that there will always be challenges in the Christian life.

It is James's exhortation, however, that strikes us as being so unexpected, and so deeply counter-cultural. For he urges us to see trials as reasons for joy. Yet here, as in the rest of his teaching, he is simply giving expression to the apostolic pattern and model. When the apostles had been beaten and warned never again to preach the gospel in Jerusalem, 'they left the presence of the council, rejoicing that they were counted worthy to suffer dishonour for the name' (Acts 5:41). They wore their suffering for Christ as a badge of honour. What a privilege to be so associated with Jesus that they were treated in the same way he had been.

These Christians had obviously experienced suffering of various kinds. We can therefore anticipate that James's teaching will be relevant to many different situations in our lives. We know that the early Christians suffered much and lost much. These particular correspondents had experienced the deprivations of exile and personal impoverishment. It is likely that they had been disinherited by their families (as perhaps the apostle Paul also was, Phil. 3:8). They had suffered the loss of the old order of life. The question for them, then, was how could they respond to James's summons 'Count it all joy'? We ask the same question ourselves.

[4]

TRIALS AS JOY?

James gives us a clue to the answer in the verb he uses: 'Count it …' (1:2).

The fact that he uses an active verb in the imperative (command) mood is an important lesson. We can easily develop a tendency to become defensive, passive, self-protective, or even defeated whenever things go against us. How we react to trials is often just as significant as the trials themselves. Hence James tells us we need to learn to count properly, to develop a biblical and divine logic. He is not urging on us the power of either wishful thinking or positive thinking. No. Rather, we are to engage in a biblical form of counting! In that sense we are to give thought to 'the bottom line' in our experience.

So, James is not a masochist. He is not telling us to take pleasure in pain. Our joy is found not in how much a trial hurts but in what it produces in us. Here James shares the same perspective on sufferings as the apostle Paul (and even uses the same verb—Rom. 5:3; 2 Cor. 4:17).

But how do we 'count it all joy …'?

Biblical accounting means we see the parts in the light of the whole. We ask, 'What does all this add up to in God's plan and design?' That requires us to think about our trials in the light of the bigger picture of God's purposes. Thus, James teaches us to ask questions about what God's test produces. The issue for the Christian is to come to the realization that through trials God means to do something to us, for us, in us, and through us. Knowledge and understanding are therefore essential for us as Christians if we are to rejoice in the face of trials.

Trials are sore, but in the divine economy their function is the 'testing of … faith'. They are always intended to prove the authenticity of our faith and to strengthen it. It is not that we count them joyful in themselves. Christians are not masochists; there is no virtue in pain and suffering for its own sake. The joy comes not from the pain but from its product. Thus, believers are to 'Count it all joy … for you know that the testing of your faith produces …' This is the consistent teaching of the New Testament. The Christian can rejoice in suffering knowing that it produces character (Rom. 5:3-4). Indeed, it is the raw material out of which glory is produced in our lives (Rom. 8:17-18; 2 Cor. 4:17-18). Tested and tried faith will 're-sult in praise and glory and honour at the revelation of Jesus Christ' (1 Pet. 1:6-7). The fire of the refiner purifies the gold-standard faith of the believer (Mal. 3:3; Job 23:10).

In this letter, James says that the testing of our faith produces steadfastness. The word he uses (*hupomonē*, 1:3; cf. 1:12; 5:11) has at its root the idea of having the ability to 'remain under' something (a weight, or a burden of some kind). It is the ability to take the strain and remain standing under a load that could crush you. Picture an Olympic weightlifter, snatching the heavily laden bar and raising it above his head, his legs shuddering until he manages to lock them into position and the judge signals a successful lift. That kind of strength is the result of endless hours of testing and more testing, and years of consistent strength-training. Here pain is gain. So it is in the Christian life. There is no other way to grow in spiritual strength than by 'the testing of your faith'. This, significantly is for Paul what turns someone into a mature Christian (Titus 2:2). It is what makes a man or woman reliable—someone you know can take the pressure and the strain and not collapse under it.

The ultimate goal, however, is not steadfastness but what it in turn produces: it proves our faith; it polishes our graces; it causes faith to shine in the world in the face of adversity. It shows that trust in Christ is not merely an insurance policy to protect us from harm, sorrow, or danger, but a joyful reliance on the Saviour who proves himself to us in all circumstances.

The Christian maturity which trials produce then makes us steady in a storm (1:6); it means that we are not distracted or diverted but single-minded (1:7-8); it means that we will not be easily taken in but be Christians with real discernment (1:16); it means that we will be able to focus on the needs of others rather than being taken up with our own well-being (1:27).

This is 'the testing of your faith'. Its 'full effect' is to make us 'perfect and complete, lacking in nothing'—that is to say, mature, well-rounded, and healthy Christians (the word translated 'com-plete' was used in a medical context in antiquity. James wants us to enjoy a clean bill of spiritual health). Through this testing we become well-balanced and well-equipped Christians. This does not mean we become 'perfect ... lacking in nothing' in the sense of being sinless (although one day that will be true). But we will be 'fit for work', as it were, able to live a healthy and fruitful Christian life.

There is no way to avoid various kinds of trials if we are to grow to spiritual maturity. Stress not only tests but also increases our resilience and reliability. If we see that, then we will understand why James tells us, in the face of trials, to 'Count it all joy, my brothers.'

2

Asking for Wisdom

*If any of you lacks wisdom, let him ask God, who gives gener-
ously to all without reproach, and it will be given him. ⁶ But
let him ask in faith, with no doubting, for the one who doubts
is like a wave of the sea that is driven and tossed by the wind.
⁷ For that person must not suppose that he will receive anything
from the Lord; ⁸ he is a double-minded man, unstable in all his
ways.*

*⁹ Let the lowly brother boast in his exaltation, ¹⁰ and the rich
in his humiliation, because like a flower of the grass he will pass
away. ¹¹ For the sun rises with its scorching heat and withers the
grass; its flower falls, and its beauty perishes. So also will the
rich man fade away in the midst of his pursuits.*

(James 1:5-11)

I magine for a moment that you have been asked to take a Word
Association Test based on your reading of the letter of James. The
administrator of the test will say a word and you are asked to respond
with the first word that comes into your head. The first three words
are: (i) 'Lord'—to which you answer 'Jesus'; (ii) 'Dispersion'—to
which you respond, 'Twelve Tribes'; and (iii) 'Testing'—and you
respond, 'Steadfastness'.

But then follows a fourth word: 'Trials'. How would you respond? The natural response is surely something like 'pain' or
'sorrow'. But James wants to teach us that the biblically instructed
Christian says: 'joy' (1:2).

What explains this association of trials and joy?

The answer is 'wisdom' (1:5). That is what we need if we are to
find joy in our trials. But such wisdom does not come all-at-once at

our regeneration. We gain it progressively. And if we are to develop it we need to ask God for it. And this in turn means recognizing that by nature I am someone who lacks wisdom.

We can explore the teaching James provides here by asking three questions.

WHAT IS 'WISDOM'?

The context gives us our first clue. James is discussing how the Christian life is marked by 'trials of various kinds'. Of course, I may try to avoid suffering; but I cannot control it. Indeed, it will inevitably come to me if I am a follower of Jesus the Suffering Servant. I therefore need (i) to learn to understand its role and (ii) to know how to respond to it practically. Only then will I be able to 'Count it all joy' (1:2). For this we need not only knowledge but the particular kind of knowledge the Bible describes as 'wisdom'—which involves not only *knowing about* but *knowing how to*. A chemistry master may fully understand the scientific information he communicates to his students; but in the laboratory his experiments may go disastrously wrong. A theological student may graduate at the head of his class and yet be a failure as a pastor. Both know a great deal but do not have a great deal of know-how.

Thus wisdom—which is embodied in an entire *genre* in the Old Testament (the books of Job, Proverbs and Ecclesiastes are of this kind)—is not merely information about life in an ideal world but knowing how to navigate life as it is in the real world with all its problems and loose ends. It is not a body of information so much as an understanding, a developed instinct, that enables us to plot a path through life so that we can be faithful to God, live in accordance with his word, and be fruitful in his service.

God himself embodies such wisdom. He expressed it in the wonders of his creation (Prov. 3:19) and he displays it in his providence. In particular he reveals his wisdom in the way in which he provides salvation—through the death of Christ—which is weakness and folly to the world, but the wisdom and the power of God for the salvation of sinners. Only one who is all-wise as well as all-powerful knows how to save sinners while remaining perfectly righteous—through the cross (1 Cor. 1:18-31).

God wants his children to walk in wisdom (Eph. 5:15). That was as true in the Old Testament as in the New. Hence, embedded in the opening chapters of the book of Proverbs we find a series of father-son talks which encourage us to develop 'the fear of the Lord' which is 'the beginning of wisdom' (Prov. 9:10). This is rooted in a basic principle: 'Trust in the LORD with all your heart, and do not lean on your own understanding. In all your ways acknowledge him, and he will make straight your paths. Be not wise in your own eyes; fear the LORD, and turn away from evil. It will be healing to your flesh and refreshment to your bones' (Prov. 3:5-8).

Wisdom is important. But what is the connection in James's thinking between trials and wisdom? The answer is that those who experience trials and temptations need wisdom if they are to discern God's purposes. This is especially true if we find ourselves handling difficult circumstances or difficult people. Wisdom sees beyond the immediate situation and looks towards God's goal. It understands that hardships are part of his child-training programme (Heb. 12:5-11—the author uses that language in 12:7, 10 and 11). This enables us in turn to yield to the Father's hand. No wonder Proverbs urges us: 'Get wisdom' (Prov. 4:5, 7).

But this raises an important question:

HOW DO WE GET WISDOM?

We 'ask God' for it (1:5). Such a request implies a recognition that we lack it, and that we see the folly of leaning on our own understanding. This involves 'acting faith' (to use a once-commonplace expression among Christians)—that is, our faith is active in consciously and deliberately focusing on God, and resting in his faithfulness and his word. We grow in wisdom when, trusting him, we learn to be submissive to his word and ways, and live in prayerful dependence upon him.

Wisdom is found in God's word. It does not come 'second-hand' as it were, merely by reading other people's wisdom in books. It cannot be learned by rote. Nor is it a matter of our IQ. Rather it involves an ongoing process of meditating on God's revelation, and applying it to our lives, watching how it works, all the while becoming increasingly sensitive to the application of its truth.

If this seems beyond us, James urges us to remember the kind of God in whom we trust: he is one who 'gives generously' and does so 'without reproach'. Indeed, he delights in his children when they tell him how frail and inexperienced they are and come to him for his help. For he is a true Father, the model father. He works everything together for the good of his people as well as for his own glory. If he has that degree of wisdom, then he has wisdom enough to help us!

This leads us to a question: Is this how we view God? Older writers used to ask: How do you 'eye' God?—meaning, what do you see when you look into his face? Does your confidence in his goodness and love depend on your circumstances? Or do you see him in the light of the self-revelation and proof of his love for you at Calvary (Rom. 5:8), as the one 'who gives generously to all without reproach' (1:5)? This is what faith grasps. It must be our starting place. Otherwise we will be exposed to the lies of the serpent in Eden that God is not generous, and in fact is a God who reproaches his children (Gen. 3:1-5).

James clearly thinks that it is a great thing to have wisdom, even if we face many obstacles to possessing it.

WHAT HINDERS US?

Why would we fail to get wisdom? James puts his finger on the issue: *doubt*. Wisdom is given when we 'ask in faith, with no doubting' (1:6). Without this, we will never enjoy the stability and poise wisdom brings: 'for the one who doubts is like a wave of the sea that is driven and tossed by the wind' (1: 6-7).

This is a vivid picture of the person who is 'double-minded' (1:8). Think of Simon Peter. In your mind's eye watch him on the night he saw Jesus on the Sea of Galilee. 'Lord,' he says, 'if it is you, command me to come to you on the water' (Matt. 14:28). For a moment he trusts in Jesus and walks towards him. But then he *sees* the wind (Matt. 14:30) and begins to sink. Matthew's choice of verb is interesting. Wind is invisible. Peter has developed double vision. Jesus is perfectly visible right there beside him, but it is the invisible wind he sees! The confidence that came from keeping his eyes fixed on Jesus disappears. What a picture of the man who is 'double-minded, unstable in all his ways' (1:8). One eye is on the promise, the other eye on the circumstances—and then both eyes are fixed on the circumstances alone! We see and hear and feel the waves; the word of promise is drowned out. We begin to walk by sight, not by faith. And as a result, we begin to sink.

The double-minded person clings to his own wisdom for security, will not receive the wisdom of God, and in the end lacks both wisdom and security. 'For that person must not suppose that he will receive anything from the Lord' (1:7).

What then is the problem with the double-minded man? He tends to trust when he sees things are going well, when he feels no special need for wisdom. He trusts God as good and wise, because life is good. His assurance that God loves him is based on the blessings he is experiencing. But this is folly. This kind of thinking contains a fatal implication rooted in an unbiblical foundation. For what happens to such 'faith' when things begin to go badly? Spiritual myopia is content with the evidence of circumstances that give us immediate happiness. But wisdom learns contentment from the knowledge that happiness is possible only when it is accompanied by holiness. And holiness is not easily produced. Purification takes place through fire (cf. 1 Pet. 1:6-7).

How then did James himself get this wisdom? It may be helpful to notice two influences that are woven into the warp and woof of the fabric of his letter.

(i) *He learned wisdom from the word of God.* He read about it in the 'sacred writings' that made him 'wise for salvation' (2 Tim. 3:15). That was true in terms of his appreciation for biblical precepts, like the book of Proverbs. But it was also true of biblical people. The pathway to wisdom was written large in the experience of a Joseph, or a David. Our lives are lived in small print, as it were, by comparison. In contrast, their lives appear to have been written in capital letters. But that enables us to read with ease and clarity in their stories the principles God regularly employs in the lives of all his people.

(ii) But no doubt *James had also come to see wisdom embodied in his half-brother.* There are, of course, two views of the family of Joseph and Mary. One view is that the children were all the offspring of their union; the other that Joseph had been married, but his wife had died, leaving him with several children. If the latter is true, then it is possible that James was older than Jesus. He would have seen how 'Jesus increased in wisdom and in stature and in favour with God and man' (Luke 2:52). But in either case, this would have been true in the years in which Jesus developed from a twelve-year-old to a thirty-year-old (Luke 2:42 and 3:23). James would therefore have seen the wisdom of God embodied in Jesus himself, and learned what it is by a kind of osmosis, by simply being near him. So with us today. The more we read of him, reflect on him, grow in love towards him, the more we become like him. This is one of the ways God gives us wisdom.

Wisdom is by no means a 'showy' quality. It does not require a large stage for its performance. Today it is uncommon to hear someone described as 'wise'. But for that very reason wisdom is one of the most important things we could ask for. Those who possess it always exercise a much-needed ministry.

James now takes up a theme that, at first sight, might seem disconnected. He writes about 'the lowly brother' (1:9) and 'the rich' man. But there is a deep connection to what he has just said. For wisdom recalibrates our value system. It creates a stunningly counter-cultural reality: a poor person ('the lowly brother') boasting in the exaltation he has experienced while all 'the rich' boast in is actually humiliation. This is true whether 'the rich' here are Christians or unbelievers. James reverses the values of our culture. Whichever we consider ourselves to be, he has wisdom to teach us.

But this wisdom is very surprising. Frequently in the New Testament boasting is seen as a symptom of a sinful heart (Rom. 1:30). Paul was concerned to see boasting die in us (see Rom. 3:27). And yet he also knows of a boasting that is produced by the gospel, a boasting in the cross and in the privileges it brings (Gal. 6:14). This paradox was already hinted at in the teaching of the Old Testament: 'Let not the wise man boast in his wisdom, let not the mighty man boast in his might, let not the rich man boast in his riches, but let him who boasts boast in this, that he understands and knows me, that I am the LORD ...' (Jer. 9:23-24).

James believed that the lowly participated in this God-centred boasting. The knowledge of God in Jesus Christ is the most satisfying treasure; by it the poor man who has nothing is exalted.

This is a profoundly counter-intuitive way of looking at what it means to be a Christian. It is worth exploring in more detail.

THE EXALTATION OF THE LOWLY

The lowly brother is encouraged to 'boast in his exaltation'. Is James purveying a sanitized form of Karl Marx's view that religion is the opiate of the people? Are these words a delusion, or at best the power of positive thinking?

James is not suggesting that poverty in itself is a good thing. Indeed, it is one of the 'trials of various kinds' to which he refers, and it can test our faith (1:2-3). Nor is he saying that the lowly brother is to boast either because of his poverty or because the gospel delivers him from poverty. Jesus (ever the realist) said that the poor would always be with us (Matt. 26:11). The gospel is not a justification for a Marxist economic strategy of wealth redistribution—although the early church understood that it transforms the way we live in the church family (Acts 2:44—which, in the light of Peter's words in Acts 5:4, can hardly be used as an argument for the illegitimacy of private ownership).

Rather the gospel brings the poor to realize that they have received true riches in Christ that transform even their poverty. They learn how to be abased, to do all things in Christ, and thus to be content (Phil. 4:11-13).

James well understood that the human heart is a 'perpetual factory of idols' (to use a telling phrase of John Calvin, *Institutes* I.xi.8). It is not only the rich that are obsessed with wealth. The poor dream of it too. Think of the popularity of lotteries which feed on that fact. Jesus' words are applicable to us all: 'the cares of the world, and the deceitfulness of riches, and the desires for other things enter in and choke the word, and it proves unfruitful' (Mark 4:19). These 'desires for other things' choke the word because our hearts and our treasure tend to occupy the same space (Matt. 6:21).

We must not misunderstand James. He is not teaching that those who have wealth can ignore the poverty of others with a free conscience. Later he will excoriate anyone who has that attitude (see 2:15-17). Nor is he speaking here about the attitude of the rich and poor to each other; rather, he is focusing only on the disposition of a poor believer. While poor in the possessions of this world, he or she may be rich in the true treasure of the kingdom of God.

Does this seem a strange calculus? Have you never met Christians from the majority or two-thirds world whose joy in Christ and whose sense of the privileges of grace have made you feel spiritually impoverished by comparison, and whose love for the Lord Jesus makes you feel unfit to tie their shoe laces?

Such wealth is to be envied. But it does not come cheap—especially if we are comparatively rich.

THE HUMILIATION OF THE RICH

James also addresses 'the rich'. Although some have held that he is addressing rich Christians here, this seems unlikely given the language he uses. He speaks of his humiliation and notes that he will pass away (1:10) and fade away in the midst of his pursuits (1:11). The heart of the man who trusts in riches is thus exposed. He has given his soul in exchange for wealth that will not endure. For a man's treasure does not consist in the abundance of his possessions but in his knowledge of God (Matt 6:19; cf. Jer. 9:23-24).

The gospel shows the rich that they have been deceived if they have trusted in riches, for what they have counted as of supreme worth has no true and lasting value at all. This is the ultimate miscalculation: the temporal has blinded them to the value of the eternal, appearances have blinded them to reality. Put a small coin to your eye and it fills your vision; it is all you can see. A penny can obscure a treasure of unimagined value! Alas for us if we are like the man John Bunyan pictures in *The Pilgrim's Progress*—raking in the mud for treasure but not seeing that someone stands before him holding a crown of gold. How sad it is that we give our hearts to the visible and material, not to the invisible and eternal! So, at least, the rich young ruler found it to be (Luke 18:23).

James presses home his point by stressing our frailty here: 'Like a flower of the grass he [the rich] will pass away' (1:10). Yet this truth is written all over the Scriptures, if only we had eyes to see and ears to hear.

> A voice says, 'Cry!'
> And I said, 'What shall I cry?'

All flesh is grass,
    and all its beauty is like the flower of the field.
The grass withers, the flower fades
    when the breath of the LORD blows on it;
    surely the people are grass (Isa. 40:6-7).

For they will soon fade like the grass
    and wither like the green herb (Psa. 37:2).

He comes out like a flower and withers;
    he flees like a shadow and continues not (Job 14:2).

Jesus exposes the folly of being rich but not being 'rich towards God'. For the day will come when the question is asked: 'the things you have prepared, whose will they be?' (Luke 12:20-21). On that day the rich man will 'fade away in the midst of his pursuits' (1:11).

What is the remedy? It is to see life from the perspective of the future, and, as it were, to live it forwards from that future. Moses is an Old Testament exemplar. He 'considered the reproach of Christ greater wealth than the treasures of Egypt, for he was looking to the reward' (Heb. 11:26). The gospel teaches us to see time in the light of eternity, and the riches of this world as mere baubles by comparison with the treasures of the world to come (2 Cor. 4:17-18).

This too is the teaching of James's Lord. Remember the parable of the Rich Fool (Luke 12:13-21)? The rich man was getting ready to sign a contract on a major expansion programme that would further his extraordinary success and be a profitable economic investment. What he did not grasp was that he was writing the last words of his own obituary notice:

> *Farmer*, Rich. Died, suddenly and unexpectedly at home in bed, under strange circumstances, and on the very day he was preparing to apply for planning permission to demolish his already substantial barns and to build larger ones for his rapidly expanding business … Friends commented on the fact that when they were with Rich earlier in the day he seemed distracted and said he thought he heard a voice saying the word 'Fool' to him. In the evening, his family said, he just seemed to fade away.

In the West it has become commonplace for eulogies to be delivered at funeral services. People are encouraged to wear bright clothes to 'celebrate' the person's life with good humour. Being serious about eternal issues is no longer socially acceptable. Rarely is a word spoken about faith in Christ, about how, though poor in this world's goods, the loved one had found lasting treasure; or how, though rich in this world's goods he or she counted everything as loss in comparison to knowing Christ (Phil 3:7-9)—and rejoiced to be part of Christ's church, mingling with rich and poor alike as a 'brother' to both. Instead people are committed, 'ashes to ashes, dust to dust', to the destiny of eternal paupers.

Do you think you have wisdom? When did you last ask for it? Have you ever asked for it? Do you realize how much you need it? Has it made a difference to your attitude to riches and poverty?

3

Understanding Temptation

*Blessed is the man who remains steadfast under trial, for when
he has stood the test he will receive the crown of life, which God
has promised to those who love him. ¹³ Let no one say when
he is tempted, 'I am being tempted by God', for God cannot be
tempted with evil, and he himself tempts no one. ¹⁴ But each
person is tempted when he is lured and enticed by his own desire.
¹⁵ Then desire when it has conceived gives birth to sin, and sin
when it is fully grown brings forth death.*

*¹⁶ Do not be deceived, my beloved brothers. ¹⁷ Every good
gift and every perfect gift is from above, coming down from the
Father of lights with whom there is no variation or shadow due
to change. ¹⁸ Of his own will he brought us forth by the word
of truth, that we should be a kind of firstfruits of his creatures.
¹⁹ Know this, my beloved brothers.*

(James 1:12-19a)

James has been writing about the trials of life. From an exclusively
this-world perspective we try to avoid them as much as possible.
But from a biblical and eternal perspective we see that they have an
important function: 'the testing of your faith' (1:3). And they have
a significant effect and goal: 'that you may be perfect [mature] and
complete, lacking in nothing' (1:4). They produce 'steadfastness'
(1:3) and eventually that in turn leads to receiving 'the crown of
life' (1:12). Thus, trials may not be pleasant, but God means them
to be productive. Having that perspective on them makes all the
difference in the world (as well as in the world to come).

So, the first words of this section encourage us once more to begin at the end and to see the present in the light of the future.

But trials come in 'various kinds' (1:2). The Christian's great need is for 'steadfastness' (1:3, 4, 12). His great encouragement is that when 'he has stood the test he will receive the crown of life, which God has promised to those who love him' (1:12). Yes, there is a test; but there is also a promise. A crown is on offer to all who love God! It consists in life—the eternal life of knowing God in Jesus Christ through the Spirit (cf. John 10:27-30; 17:3). Place that in the scales over against our present trials and they will seem light by comparison (2 Cor. 4:17).

Thus far James has been focused on suffering, on trials that come in the form of privation. The beatitude he pronounces in verse 12 ('Blessed is the man who remains steadfast under trial') seems to act as a bridge within his discussion. It looks back to what he had said in 1:2-4 and gives an ultimate reason for joy in the face of suffering. But it also opens this section with its new focus. For 'trials' (1:2) also take the form of temptation. The prospect of the crown of life enables us to remain steadfast (1:3-4). But it also motivates us to resist temptation. To this sub-theme James now turns in an extended and very important discussion.

James first clears up a potential confusion in our thinking. All trials and testing come to us in the providence of God. He uses them to transform us as we respond to them in faith and with biblical insight. But we must distinguish God's providential ordering of temptations from the mistaken idea that God himself tempts us and therefore, by implication, bears responsibility for our failure and sin. No blame-shifting is allowed here (as is already clear in the events recorded in Genesis 3, where Adam sought to shift the blame for his sin to Eve and, by implication, to the Lord himself).

James is emphatic: 'God cannot be tempted with evil, and he himself tempts no one. But each person is tempted when he is lured and enticed by his own desire' (1:13-14). But exactly what is he addressing here? This truth is surely too obvious to need to be stated. Yet this is virtually what Adam said to the Lord in his blame-shifting attempt to cover his own failure: 'The woman whom you gave to be with me, she gave me fruit of the tree and I ate' (Gen. 3:12). And the human heart is sufficiently subtle to create new versions of the same self-justification: 'If it were not for these things that happened in the providence of God, I would never have ... . So, it isn't entirely my fault.' The implication is that God must bear his share of the responsibility. James will have none of it. God is not the author of sin. He may well test the quality of his workmanship; but he never solicits us to sin. To imagine he does so is a perverse distortion of his character (1:13, 16).

With this clarification in mind we are ready to grapple with James's teaching on the nature of temptation and how it works, and on what the Christian needs to know to be defended against it.

HOW TEMPTATION WORKS

Temptation often creeps up on us unnoticed. How often someone will confess after grievous sin, 'I don't know what came over me. I don't understand what I must have been thinking. I wasn't thinking … I didn't realize ….' Without explaining to us all the implications of his thinking, James displays remarkable shrewdness in his approach to this subject. His teaching is a model not only of solid doctrinal exposition but also of important pastoral strategies.

Temptation may seem to overcome us in a moment in time, but it always exhibits a very definite pattern. James is here teaching us how to recognize it. He does this by a careful analysis of how it works.

Think of a televised sporting event. A goal is scored in a soccer match, there is a marvellous play in a basketball game, or a young professional golfer holds his nerve to play an amazing shot from a hundred yards to within inches of the hole. Then, with the aid of high-tech equipment, what seemed to take place in a moment in time is replayed slowly. The sports analyst points out the skills involved, discusses, for example, how the golfer managed to put so much backspin on his golf ball that although it took a couple of bounces forward when it landed it then spun back along the grass as though he were pulling it on an invisible string. Now you understand that what happened in an instant was the product of an entire series of actions.

The same is true of temptation. Here James slows down the single moment when temptation takes hold of us. He leads us frame by frame through an analysis of how it works. It is as though he were saying 'Look at this! See this! Watch out for this happening!' To change the metaphor, he puts temptation under the microscope so that we can learn to recognize elements in it we might not otherwise notice. In this way he is developing in us an awareness of how subtle temptation actually is.

We might call James 1:14-15 'The Temptation Cycle'.

THE TEMPTATION CYCLE

We can break down this cycle into the following stages:

(i) Deception

The goal Satan has in view in all temptation is our deception (he is, after all, the 'deceiver', Rev. 12:9; 13:14). James does not mention being 'deceived' until the end of the section (1:16). But it is worth remembering the principle of the Greek philosopher Aristotle, that the last thing we have in view as our goal must be the first thing in mind in setting our strategy; the goal determines everything that leads to it. So here, the Tempter means to deceive us. But he will do this by blinding us and confusing us so that we neither think nor see clearly. It should not surprise us then when we hear someone who has sinned grievously saying, 'I don't know what I was thinking.' That was precisely the Deceiver's goal. Temptation to sin involves a blurring of the mind to reality. We do not think clearly enough, or see far enough to ask the question, Where will this lead?

Paul says this happened in the first temptation: 'Adam was not deceived, but the woman was deceived and became a transgressor' (1 Tim. 2:14). This may seem to be the statement of a misogynist, but in fact it is essentially a quotation from Eve herself: 'The woman said, "The serpent deceived me, and I ate"' (Gen. 3:13). And how was she deceived? Through assessing reality by looking and seeing things through her eyes, rather than hearing them interpreted by God's word and listening to it through her ears. Every day we need to have this watchword before us 'Do not be deceived! Remember to see with your ears!'

(ii) Attraction

What carries no attraction for us rarely deceives us. We are tempted only by what we find attractive. James speaks about being 'lured' (1:14). Fishermen know all about lures—that 'fly' on the end of the fishing line hides a vicious little hook, but it is so attractive to the naïve fish.

We cannot afford to be naïve. God has made everything beautiful in its season, but each thing for its own purpose (Eccles. 3:11). The tree of the knowledge of good and evil in the Garden of Eden looked 'good for food, and … a delight to the eyes' (Gen. 3:6). Genesis has already informed us that this was true of all the trees God made; they were 'pleasant to the sight and good for food' (Gen. 2:9). But the serpent's subtle innuendoes about God's restrictiveness led Eve to see something else in the tree of the knowledge of good and evil. This tree was now 'to be desired to make one wise'. Here attraction proved fatal. She now saw the tree in its own light rather than in the light of God's word. Now everything about the tree seemed to say to her 'take and eat' as though this were the way to wisdom.

In stark contrast God had said, 'Do not take and do not eat—for by obedience to me you will surely grow in wisdom and holiness. Obey me, Adam and Eve, simply because I am your gracious Father, and I have your best interests at heart. Show me that you trust and love me by not eating from this tree—just because that is my command. Seek first my kingdom and righteousness and everything else will be yours!'

But Eve swallowed the lure, both metaphorically and literally. Something had happened: attraction had led to—

(iii) Preoccupation

Once allured, we are easily 'enticed'. It is as though what was once outside of us has come inside, and we can no longer get it back out.

Peter has a striking way of describing this when he speaks about people who 'have eyes full of adultery' (2 Pet. 2:14); but it could be other things. Temptation to sin is now no longer external to us. It has successfully invaded us. What fills our vision now is the thought of the object of our desire and how to make it ours. Our mind has been gripped and our affections captured by it. We have swallowed the bait. What began as an external attraction has now become an internal preoccupation. At first, we were drawn away to it; but now we need it; we will not be content without it.

Up to this point we could easily believe that the scene of Genesis 2-3 is playing in the background of James's mind. But now he uses a verb that makes us fast forward from the Garden of Eden to a later scene in the Old Testament.

(iv) Conception

'Then desire when it has conceived ...' (1:15). The sperm of temptation unites with the egg of opportunity. Sometimes we experience a sinful desire, but no opportunity arises for its exercise. And sometimes the opportunity arises when we are not overtaken by desire. But when desire and opportunity coalesce, and we yield to what has preoccupied our minds, then conception takes place.

With the sudden interjection of this verb, 'conceive', our minds are shifted from Eve in Genesis 2–3 to 2 Samuel 11–12 and the story of David's adultery with Bathsheba. There, as in Genesis 3, the author slows down the action and analyses it into its constituent parts: 'It happened ... he saw ... sent ... enquired ... took ... And the woman conceived' (2 Sam. 11:2-5). Notice the cycle: deception, attraction, preoccupation, conception. David would never be the same man again. And all because instead of being 'out to battle' as a king, he was lying on his couch on the roof of his house (2 Sam. 11:1-2). The person who neglects his or her God-given calling and responsibilities exposes himself or herself to the possibility that they will soon neglect God's most basic commandments.

John Bunyan said it as well as anybody could:

> Sin rather than 'twill out of action be
> Will pray to stay, though but a while with thee,
> One night, one hour, one moment, will it cry,
> Embrace me in thy bosom, else I die.
> Time to repent (saith it) I will allow,
> And help, if to repent thou know'st not how.
> But if you give it entrance at the door,
> It will come in and may go out no more.[1]

(v) Subjection

Temptation is like the weaving of a spider's web; it is much more than an isolated event. And it brings our whole lives into subjection. It is never truer than it is here that 'one thing leads to another': 'sin when it is fully grown brings forth death' (1:15).

---

[1] John Bunyan, 'A Caution to Stir Up Watch against Sin' (London: 1684), verse 2.

David's adultery (if only he had 'seen' with his ears!) developed into the 'cover-up' that involved the death of Bathsheba's husband, the brave and noble Uriah (2 Sam. 11:6-27). Although not 'one of the three' mighty men in David's confidence, he was nevertheless one of 'the thirty' (2 Sam. 23:8-39). His integrity contrasts sharply with David's fall as he descended into despicable actions.

As if to underline the cycle of tragedy David initiated, we learn Bathsheba's son (who is never named in Scripture) died (2 Sam. 12:15-23). Sin indeed 'brings forth death'. No wonder the author of Hebrews encourages us to 'exhort one another every day, as long as it is called "today", that none of you may be hardened by the deceitfulness of sin' (Heb. 3:13). James puts it more bluntly: 'Do not be deceived, my beloved brothers' (1:16).

At first reading we could easily think that these verses are simply descriptive. The only prescriptive element in them appears to be the book-end exhortations, 'Let no one say when he is tempted "I am being tempted by God"' (1:13), and 'Do not be deceived, my beloved brothers' (1:16). But there is more to this than meets the eye at first reading. For James displays a characteristic that is common to the apostles. Enshrined in the descriptive is the prescriptive. Woven into the warp and woof of the indicative statements (describing the *what*) we can find a series of imperatives (answering the question *how?*). So, we must now ask: *What are the safeguards that will enable us to remain steadfast?* We must not be ignorant of Satan's devices (2 Cor. 2:11). But nor should we be ignorant of the safeguards the gospel provides for us.

REMAINING STEADFAST

Enshrined then in James's words are four vital principles.

1. *Be familiar with the Temptation Cycle.* Here knowledge is power: 'A wise man is full of strength, and a man of knowledge enhances his might' (Prov. 24:5). James has been supplying us with valuable spiritual understanding in the patient and careful way he has explained the dynamics of temptation. He has been slowing its action down, showing us frame by frame how it works, teaching us that deception is the end game of attraction, preoccupation and conception. And he has underlined that it leads to death. Knowing this gives us insight, enables us to develop an intuitive sense of what

is happening to us, helps us to recognize amber warning lights, and encourages us always to ask the questions 'What is really going on under the surface of appearances here?' and 'Where will this end?'

But we need more than knowledge; we need conviction. This explains why—in what may seem to be a disconnected statement—James directs our attention to—

2. *The unchanging goodness of God.* Here is bedrock. What protects us from being deceived is the conviction that our Father is good, through and through. He is altogether good, permanently good, and all he does is good, and good for us: 'Every good gift and every perfect gift is from above, coming down from the Father of lights with whom there is no variation or shadow due to change' (1:17).

James was too wise a pastor to pause here and say, 'Now what you need from me is a theology lesson.' But it would be remiss of us if we failed to notice (i) that this is exactly what he is giving us, and (ii) why it is important at the practical level. In the process he is once more giving the lie to the naïve view that the value of his letter is that he is so practical and not at all theological.

(i) How we think about God is the foundation of the Christian life (John 17:3) and influences everything we are, say, and do—even although we often do not realize it. What does James want us to know about him, to be convinced of in our minds and to permeate our affections? Notice his carefully chosen language. He is 'Father'. All things owe their creation to him. He was the Father of God's people (Mal. 1:6) in the sense that he brought them into being at the Exodus. He has become our Father in giving us new life (1:18; 1 Pet. 1:3). He cares for us as our Father in heaven (Matt. 6:9, 14-15, 18, 26, 32). And here James also calls him 'the Father of lights', probably referring to the heavenly lights and especially the sun and the moon (Gen 1:3, 14-19). But he chooses this unique expression to emphasize the idea of light in distinction from darkness. There is 'no variation' in him. He is the unchangeable God. He always is everything he is. This is terrifying to an unbeliever, but it is the security of the believer (Mal. 3:6). And there is 'no shadow' in him. There is no dark side in God.

(ii) Why is this so important? Because this knowledge of God guards us against the subtle nature of Satan's deceptive wiles. They are as old as the Garden of Eden, and perhaps older still if we consider his leadership of an angelic rebellion against God. His scarcely disguised innuendo to Eve in the Garden was 'Has he set you in this wonderful world, full of attractive, delicious fruit trees and told you "You shall not eat of any tree in the garden"?' (Gen. 3:1). That innuendo is present in every temptation—the subtle implication that God is not as good as he seems; indeed, there is a streak of malice in him; he does not desire what is best for you—but you can have that simply by taking it yourself: so, take and eat! Jesus himself faced the same strategy when weak, hungry and thirsty in the wilderness ('Surely if God is really good he doesn't want this for you, only to be followed by death on the cross? Come now, Jesus, turn the stones into bread—take and eat!').

Only the conviction that God is unqualified goodness and will work everything together for our good gives us the strength we need to resist.

'Do not be deceived.' The addiction into which the Deceiver seeks to draw us is a banquet of death. By contrast our heavenly Father spreads a banquet of life for us 'in the presence of our enemies'. He makes our cup run over. We will say therefore: Surely your goodness will pursue us all the days of our lives and we will dwell in your house for ever (cf. Psa. 23:5-6).

Not only is this true, but it carries a corollary.

3. *God gives us the transforming power of a new birth* (1:18).

What is the connection between the goodness of God in verse 17 and the statement in verse 18 that he has caused us to be born again? This: Satan seeks to cause us to despair, to convince us that we are too weak to resist him. We have failed before and we will not be able to overcome him now.

But this too is a deceptive lie. God has made us part of a new creation in Christ (2 Cor. 5:17). We have been born anew to a living hope through Christ's resurrection. Not only so, but it is 'of his own will he brought us forth'. Our regeneration is not only a work of God's sovereign power, but also of his sovereign loving choice. And this comes with the assurance that he will keep us for the inheritance he is keeping for us (1 Pet. 1:3-9; cf. Eph.1:3-13). In addition, that same power provides us with everything we need to live for God's glory (2 Pet. 1:3-11). We can therefore be sure that—

> The work which his goodness began,
> The arm of his strength will complete …

Yes, I to the end shall endure,
As sure as the earnest is given;
More happy, but not more secure,
The glorified spirits in heaven.[1]

Indeed, how marvellous that it is Simon Peter—the man who
failed so badly and was deceived more than once—who adds his
testimony to that of the exemplary James—more than that who
explains in detail the new birth about which James speaks (1 Pet.
1:3-9). What James teaches is what the weak Simon Peter experienced—and so may we.

Older Christians used to speak about the way we can 'live below
our privileges' and fail to realize what they are. James emphasizes
one of them in this context. We are 'a kind of firstfruits of his
creatures' (1:18). Later, in verse 21, he will encourage us to receive
the word of God like a seed falling into good soil. Here he mentions
the fruit of that—those who have been born again into God's family
are like the specially consecrated firstfruits of the harvest, pointing
forwards to the final harvest God will usher in at the re-creation
of all things. Indeed, says Paul a number of years later, 'the whole
creation is on tiptoe to see the wonderful sight of the sons of God
coming into their own' (Rom. 8:19, J. B. Phillips).

An important question sometimes arises in this context: if
regeneration is a *sovereign* work of God, how can it be that we are
'brought ... forth *by the word of truth*' (1:18)? Does this not imply
an active response on our part, and therefore a co-operative activity?
But there is in fact no contradiction here. The new birth involves
the illumination of our minds so that we 'see' the kingdom of God
(John 3:3)—its significance 'dawns upon us'. This does not take
place in a vacuum, nor is it simply a matter of reminding us of
what we already know. Rather, it takes place as the Spirit illumines
our understanding as he works with God's word so that we at last
'see' the truth. It is something God himself does. The fact that he
works *sovereignly* does not imply that he works *without instrumen-
tality*. Rather, as the Spirit uses the word he has inspired for us he
makes Christ known to us, and thus brings us to 'see' and to 'enter'

---

[1] From the hymn by Augustus Montague Toplady (1740–78), 'A debtor to
mercy alone'.

the kingdom of God (John 3:3, 5). We are thus 'brought …forth by the word of truth'.

If we are indeed already firstfruits, then a further implication follows—

4. *See the present in the light of the future.* James also directs our attention to a fourth principle found in the words with which he opened this section of his letter: 'Blessed is the man who remains steadfast under trial, for when he has stood the test he will receive the crown of life, which God has promised to those who love him' (1:12). Moses resisted temptation 'looking to the reward' (Heb. 11:26), not in the sense of earning it, but understanding that God had promised it. We have everything to gain by resisting temptation; we have everything to lose by yielding to it, and nothing to gain eternally by doing so. We therefore not only need to learn to slow temptation down and examine it frame by frame so that we can ask 'What is really happening here?' We need to make sure that we do this in the light of eternity.

In most of our English versions a paragraph division appears at the end of verse 18. But perhaps James's next words 'Know this, my beloved brothers' (1:19a) belong here too. If so they represent James's urgent appeal to us to make sure we are armed with the knowledge he has just given us.

4

Obeying God's Word

Know this, my beloved brothers: let every person be quick to hear, slow to speak, slow to anger; ²⁰ for the anger of man does not produce the righteousness of God. ²¹ Therefore put away all filthiness and rampant wickedness and receive with meekness the implanted word, which is able to save your souls. ²² But be doers of the word, and not hearers only, deceiving yourselves. ²³ For if anyone is a hearer of the word and not a doer, he is like a man who looks intently at his natural face in a mirror. ²⁴ For he looks at himself and goes away and at once forgets what he was like. ²⁵ But the one who looks into the perfect law, the law of liberty, and perseveres, being no hearer who forgets but a doer who acts, he will be blessed in his doing.

²⁶ If anyone thinks he is religious and does not bridle his tongue but deceives his heart, this person's religion is worthless. ²⁷ Religion that is pure and undefiled before God, the Father, is this: to visit orphans and widows in their affliction, and to keep oneself unstained from the world.

(James 1:19-27)

James is bringing the word of God to his scattered flock by means of a written sermon—perhaps even a series of outlines of various sermons he had preached. The ministry of God's word always has multi-dimensional goals. James's goal here is to encourage spiritual maturity, so that his friends will be 'perfect and complete' (1:4).

It becomes progressively clear in the letter that this maturity is developed by means of two instruments. The first, as we have seen, is through our experience of, and response to, trials and temptations.

he turns to the second: how we respond to, and work out into ur lives, the teaching of God's word. Our calling is to 'receive with meekness the implanted word' (1:21). James now underlines a point we noted in the previous section: the Christian needs to learn to 'see' through his or her ears. If we are to do this, our hearing needs to have greater powers of acceleration than our speaking: 'let every person be quick to hear, slow to speak' (1:19).

This is always a relevant exhortation. But perhaps it has a special relevance in the contemporary world when both educational methods and social media facilitate and foster the voicing of instantaneous expressions of opinion. In the world we inhabit the opposite of James's teaching is encouraged—and Christians can be caught up in the ethos of the day when it tends to be those who are quick to speak, not those who are 'quick to hear', who dominate the headlines. Not only having but expressing opinions is a major aspect of our contemporary culture. It is surely not stretching the application of James's words here to say that they also imply 'be slow to tweet'. In this—as in so many other things—the Christian should be deeply counter-cultural.

In addition, James seems to be suggesting a kind of spiritual version of Newton's First Law of Motion: a tongue at rest tends to stay at rest; but a tongue in motion tends to stay in motion! For if being 'slow to speak' means we will also be 'slow to anger', then being quick to speak carries with it the obvious danger that our tongue will lose control and begin to express the enmity in our hearts in the anger of our lips. In one of his proverb-type statements James gives us a principle: 'the anger of man does not produce the righteousness of God' (1:20).

Granted there is such an emotion as 'righteous anger'; but usually, as far as the kingdom is concerned, anger is counter-productive. It twists things further rather than straightening them out. 'Angry Christian' seems to be an oxymoron, a contradiction in terms. But regeneration does not fully and finally rid us of anger's presence (Eph. 4:31; Col.3:8). Yes, Paul hints that there may be a proper anger, but it must not fester (Eph. 4:26). If it does, while it may lie hidden under the surface, it will emerge in a disposition to criticize others, to 'put them in their place', sometimes in a sarcastic personality, sometimes in cynicism. Alas, angry Christians usually do not know themselves well enough, do not understand the jarring nature of their behaviour, and have no sense that they have spiritual bad breath. Instead they assume that they are guardians of the righteousness of God. James tells them (and us!) very bluntly that the anger of man does not produce the righteousness that God requires—either in others or in ourselves.

It is wonderful to say we 'love the Letter of James'. But it may not be wise to add 'because it is so practical rather than theological—not like Paul; he finds me where I am'. It certainly does 'find us'—but in the most searching ways. In fact, he finds us where we ourselves assume we are not! And we have seen that there is weighty theology woven into the fabric of his teaching. But here we see that James even thinks in the same theological ways as the apostle Paul. He understands how the logic of the gospel works.

This is signalled by his use of the introductory connective word 'therefore' in verse 21. He has given us a strong exhortation, one that many of us find difficult to obey: 'be quick to hear, slow to speak'. It is not a suggestion, but a command. All very well; but how?

James explains in verse 21. Here he shows himself to be a true physician of the soul, like a medical doctor who understands the principle of 'referred pain' (the source of the problem may be different from the part of the anatomy where the pain is felt). In the same way the symptoms of spiritual disease that are found on our tongues have their origin not in the mouth but in the heart! James is simply applying the teaching of his half-brother, the Lord Jesus, that it is 'out of the abundance of the heart [that] the mouth speaks' (Matt. 12:34).

This being the case, we must first deal with what walks out of our hearts and into our lives: 'put away all filthiness and rampant wickedness' (1:21). James certainly calls a spade a spade. His wisdom is seen in the fact that he does not assume that these simply disappear from our lives the moment we become believers. Were that so, large sections of the apostolic letters would never have seen the light of day. We are part of a new creation in Christ, but still living in the old world. We have been renewed, but we are recovering sin-addicts, and the remainders of indwelling sin can be very stubborn lodgers in the temple of the Spirit. So, we must 'put away' all that belonged to the old life (his verb expresses the idea of putting off old and soiled clothing. Paul also uses it in Ephesians 4:22).

But this raises another question: *How?* Here it is important to follow James closely and to notice his logic. He issues a series of practical imperatives ('be quick to hear, slow to speak …'). These are the new clothes we are to 'put on' now (cf. Eph. 4:24; Col. 3:12. The deeper we dig down into James's teaching the more we find similarities to Paul's!). Notice that this takes place not by our un-aided activity but by our receptivity to the word of God: 'receive with meekness the implanted word, which is able to save your souls' (1:21). Christ the farmer implants the seed of his word in our hearts (Mark 4:1-20). We are to receive it—'with meekness'. That is what makes us 'good soil'—when we 'let the word of Christ dwell' in us 'richly' (Col. 3:16).

We must not miss the principle here: we are active in our spiritual progress; we 'work out' our salvation; but only because 'it is God who works' in us (Phil. 2:12-13). In a letter which has so much to teach us about what we are to do, we must not miss James's emphasis on what God does. His bedrock is that God's word does its own work in us. Otherwise that word simply throws us back on resources we do not possess, and that in turn leads only to an increasing sense of frustration at our failure and a paralysis in our growth. We are called to 'receive … the implanted word' (1:21) in order that we may become 'doers of the word' (1:22). The order must never be reversed; it can never be reversed.

At the same time, James recognizes how important balance is if we are to grow to maturity in the Christian life. When we are younger Christians we rarely regard balance as important—it may even suggest compromise to us! Zeal, not balance, is the *sine qua non*! But if there is a lack of balance in our growth, we will eventually topple over—forwards, backwards, or to one side or the other! It often happens this way. We begin as activists and have little patience with doctrine. Then we are gripped by the importance of doctrine. At first *doing* was everything to us; but now *knowing* has become everything to us and we are no longer doing! James comes to our assistance and steadies us: 'receive … the … word . . . But be doers of the word' (1:21-22).

James has not left behind the concern he expressed earlier in the chapter about Christians being deceived. Now he warns against two kinds, perhaps better two dimensions, of deception. He uses two different Greek words. In verse 22 'deceiving yourselves' implies the idea of going astray; in verse 26 'deceives his heart' implies the idea of misleading ourselves. James has in view the way we can lead ourselves astray. But he also has in view a deeper dimension that may lie behind our wandering, namely the deception of the heart (1:26). Christians can be extraordinarily ingenious in persuading themselves that what they are doing must be God's will. In speaking this way, James is further developing his teaching on temptation. We have already seen that it clouds the vision with respect to sin. Now he focuses on another form of this deception involving a subtle double confusion.

1: CONFUSING HEARING WITH DOING

The language 'the implanted word' is suggestive of the word of God acting like a seed that germinates in our lives and produces its own fruit. Several New Testament authors employ this metaphor. Paul speaks about the word of God, the gospel 'bearing fruit and increasing' (Col. 1:6), of it being 'at work' in believers (1 Thess. 2:13); Luke notes that 'the word of God continued to increase' (Acts 6:7; cf. Acts 19:20).

What is James's concern here? He is warning us that it is easy to be deceived into thinking that because we hear the word we are also obeying the word. How easily, for example, we assume that if people attend a church where there is outstanding biblical preaching they are, by implication, discerning and mature Christians. But while there is a correlation between the ministry of the word and spiritual growth, it is not an automatic one. So, a subtle false logic is at work. Hearing is not necessarily the same as heart obedience. There is a phenomenon we might call 'vicarious obedience'. We assume that, since we hear rich and full biblical teaching from a preacher who has submitted his life to God's word, we ourselves are thereby also living in obedience to it.

James pulls us up short. Sadly, we can be like someone 'who looks intently at his natural face in a mirror ... and goes away and at once forgets what he was like' (1:23-24).

This is imaginary obedience. An impression has been made on us, but it does not last. The soil of our hearts is simply the pathway on which the farmer often walks; the seed of the word falls on our ears but penetrates no further. Or perhaps we are rocky or thorn-infested soil. Our faithful preacher is like Ezekiel. We come to hear him, but not to obey the word of God he expounds (Ezek. 33:30-32). We develop spiritual rickets because we are lacking in the vitamin D the word of God produces when hearing it issues in obedience. We have soft bones, large heads, and weak joints. We need to be undeceived before it is too late.

What is the cure? Verse 25 provides the answer. We need to 'take the medicine' of the word of God. There is no substitute for it if we are to be 'complete', i.e. in good spiritual health (1:4). Read the instructions Dr James has written on the label: peer into and persevere in the word of God by living it out in your life.

The verb translated 'looks into' (*parakuptō*, 1:25) conveys the idea of stooping down in order to look into, or peer into something. It is used in John 20:5 of John 'stooping to look in' the tomb in which Jesus had been buried, and in 1 Peter 1:12 of the angels longing 'to look into' the wonders of the gospel. We might paraphrase James's words by saying 'Keep your head down in the Book!'

But why does James use very distinctive language to describe God's word? He calls it 'the perfect law, the law of liberty' (1:25).

The first expression ('perfect law') echoes Psalm 19:7: the word of God is complete and can make us complete or mature. And in that process, it sets us free because it is the law of liberty. When we receive the law of God from the Son of God it brings not bondage but freedom. Those who come to him find that (in the words of the collect for peace in *The Book of Common Prayer*), his 'service is perfect freedom' (cf. Matt. 11:28-30). By the power of the Spirit what the naked law could never accomplish has been done for us by Christ and is worked into us by the Spirit (Rom. 8:3-4). In fact, James has just illustrated the point he is making here: God's word does its work in our lives not by treating us as robots but by effecting in us an obedience to its commands, and a desire to live in a way that is consistent with its precepts. We thus 'work out' what the Spirit 'works in' us through the word (Phil. 2:12-13).

This is why there needs to be persevering in obedience to the word as well as peering into it. But persevering in what?

It is sometimes said that you can tell how important a concept is in a culture by the size of the vocabulary its language has to describe it. If that is so, then in the culture of the gospel perseverance is important. James himself had already used one term (*hupomonē*, which carries the basic idea of being able to remain under something—picture someone carrying a heavy load without buckling under the weight of it). Now the verb he uses (*paramenō*) has the basic meaning of remaining alongside. It is used by Paul when he speaks about his expectation that his life would be spared so that he would be able 'to remain and continue' with the Philippians. Here, in James, the idea seems to be that we not only study and meditate on the Scripture, but we keep in step with it. So, just as Paul's exhortation to 'be filled with the Spirit' (Eph. 5:18) means letting 'the word of Christ dwell' in us 'richly' (Col. 3:16), so 'keep in step with the Spirit' (Gal. 5:25) implies 'keeping in step with the word', allowing it to dwell in us richly as he enables us to fulfil the royal law of freedom (Rom. 8:3-4).

But confusing hearing with doing is not the only way we can deceive ourselves.

2: CONFUSING TALK WITH OBEDIENCE

If it is possible to confuse listening to biblical exposition with practical Christian obedience, it is also possible to deceive ourselves into believing that because we can talk about the gospel, Scripture, theology, church history, apologetics and so on we are thereby being obedient to the gospel. Nor is this deceit limited to what might be thought of as the more doctrinal aspects of Christianity. Some people seem to be able to talk just as confidently about how the church should be shaped, what political agenda Christians should follow, and a multitude of other subjects. You name it, they have an opinion on it. Unfortunately, there is sometimes a tendency to confuse this ability with spiritual maturity, even to assume that an ability to win arguments is evidence of leadership potential.

James holds a very different view. True godliness is found in the person who can 'bridle his tongue'. Its antithesis is when our talk bridles the tongues of others. Being opinionated or being able to dominate conversations is never a mark of grace, whereas the ability to say nothing often is. The person with an unbridled tongue is a person whose 'religion is worthless', no matter how impressive it seems.

More than that, James says, such a person 'deceives his heart'. Notice his equation: Unbridled tongue = Self-deceived heart. How can this be? Because so often the person who fails to bridle his tongue mistakes that propensity for spiritual giftedness, when in fact it expresses a lack of grace. The truth about him is the reverse of what he thinks about himself.

Think of Talkative in John Bunyan's *Pilgrim's Progress*. As Faithful eventually says, when his eyes have been opened to Talkative's self-deceit:

> How *Talkative* at first lifts up his plumes!
> How bravely doth he speak! how he presumes
> To drive down all before him! but so soon
> As *Faithful* talks of *heart-work*, like the moon
> That's past the full, into the wane he goes;
> And so will all but he that *heart-work* knows.

The real issue is whether we prefer to talk about the things of God rather than do the things God says, whether knowledge of the truth is more important to us than experience of the power of the truth we know.

Remember the rather strange incident in Jesus' life when, 'As he said these things, a woman in the crowd raised her voice and said to him, "Blessed is the womb that bore you, and the breasts at which you nursed"'? Lofty theology indeed. Would this not impress Jesus, given his love for his mother Mary? But notice Jesus' response: 'But he said, "Blessed rather are those who hear the word of God and keep it!"' (Luke 11:27-28).

Are those who obey the word of God more blessed than the virgin Mary? Was this woman not simply echoing the words of Elizabeth and saying the same thing thirty years later? 'Blessed are you among women, and blessed is the fruit of your womb!' (Luke 1:42). No. It was not Mary's womb that Elizabeth pronounced blessed, but its fruit. And she herself came to share in the blessing Jesus pronounced, for she heard the word of God, saying 'I am the servant of the Lord; let it be to me according to your word' (Luke 1:38). And then she kept it, for she 'treasured up all these things, pondering them in her heart' (Luke 2:19).

But is an unbridled tongue such a serious flaw? After all, it isn't exactly breaking any of the Ten Commandments, is it? James sees it as very serious, even deadly serious. For it can easily lead to the breach of any of the commandments, and indeed to all of them. It renders our religion 'worthless' (1:26)—that is, fruitless, powerless, useless, empty, lacking in integrity. Paul uses the same word when he says that apart from the resurrection of Christ our faith is 'futile' (1 Cor. 15:17). An unbridled tongue has the same effect as an un-resurrected Christ. It is that serious.

If the mere ability to talk does not constitute 'pure and undefiled' religion, what does? Notice the implication that loose talk is not neutral in God's eyes but impure and defiled.

James provides a two-step summary. First, real Christianity means doing those things that express the heart of God—'visit orphans and widows in their affliction'. (See Deut. 10:18; 14:29; 24:19; 26:12.) Second, it implies developing a lifestyle free from this-world perspectives and a desire to draw attention to ourselves. This is what is implied in the exhortation to 'keep oneself unstained from the world' (1:27). That should show itself as an unblemished life, not an unbridled tongue. True religion is expressed in what we do among those who tend to be hidden and marginalized. After all, did not James's half-brother teach us that 'as you did it to one of *the least of these* my brothers, you did it to me' (Matt. 25:40)?

How far short we fall! How much James's words constitute a summons to repentance! But how?

His teaching suggests what we might call 'The Four Rs':

- *Receive* the word of God with meekness of spirit, saying 'Speak Lord, for your servant hears' (1 Sam. 3:9).
- *Reject* whatever is ungodly in your heart.
- *Reserve* or store up the word of God.
- *Respond* to those you see who seem to be in need.

All this is reminiscent of the parable of the Sower and the Soils (Mark 4:1-20). But it is also reminiscent of the parable with which Jesus climaxed the Sermon on the Mount: 'Everyone then who hears these words of mine and does them will be like a wise man who built his house on the rock. And the rain fell, and the floods came, and the winds blew and beat on that house, but it did not fall, because it had been founded on the rock. And everyone who hears these words of mine and does not do them will be like a foolish man who built his house on the sand. And the rain fell, and the floods came, and the winds blew and beat against that house, and it fell, and great was the fall of it' (Matt. 7:24-27).

When Jesus said, 'He who has ears to hear, let him hear' (Matt. 11:15), he was talking not only about listening but about obeying.

5

Impartiality in the Church

My brothers, show no partiality as you hold the faith in our Lord Jesus Christ, the Lord of glory. ² For if a man wearing a gold ring and fine clothing comes into your assembly, and a poor man in shabby clothing also comes in, ³ and if you pay attention to the one who wears the fine clothing and say, 'You sit here in a good place', while you say to the poor man, 'You stand over there', or, 'Sit down at my feet', ⁴ have you not then made distinctions among yourselves and become judges with evil thoughts? ⁵ Listen, my beloved brothers, has not God chosen those who are poor in the world to be rich in faith and heirs of the kingdom, which he has promised to those who love him? ⁶ But you have dishonoured the poor man. Are not the rich the ones who oppress you, and the ones who drag you into court? ⁷ Are they not the ones who blaspheme the honourable name by which you were called?

⁸ If you really fulfil the royal law according to the Scripture, 'You shall love your neighbour as yourself', you are doing well. ⁹ But if you show partiality, you are committing sin and are convicted by the law as transgressors. ¹⁰ For whoever keeps the whole law but fails in one point has become accountable for all of it. ¹¹ For he who said, 'Do not commit adultery', also said, 'Do not murder.' If you do not commit adultery but do murder, you have become a transgressor of the law. ¹² So speak and so act as those who are to be judged under the law of liberty. ¹³ For judgement is without mercy to one who has shown no mercy. Mercy triumphs over judgement.

(James 2:1-13)

I t could happen in any church. Everyone notices him as he enters with his wife ('Look at that coat! Did you see his ring?'). One of the ushers makes sure they find their seat. A member whispers to the friend who is visiting 'You know who that is, don't you? He's a member here, you know.' Meanwhile old Mr Smith came in by the side door ('Look at the width of that tie!'). People see him, but it is to the other man people 'pay attention' (2:3). Nobody takes much notice of Mr Smith, although he always seems to be there. The young people by and large ignore him. Few members know anything about him. They have never shown enough interest to ask him what his spiritual pilgrimage has been. And so, they have never heard the wonderful story of God's grace in his life.

It is all perfectly natural, perfectly understandable. No church is perfect. But that is not the verdict of Scripture. James makes a very different assessment of an analogous situation (described by him in 2:1-3). He says we have become 'judges with evil thoughts' (2:4). So, who is 'telling it the way it is'? James has already warned us about being deceived. Have we been deceived again? Is it possible that inasmuch as we have ignored old Mr Smith we may have ignored Jesus himself (cf. Matt. 25:40)?

James seems to say so. He leads us through his diagnosis and also writes a prescription to cure us of our spiritual sickness.

A PRINCIPLE ENUNCIATED

We are to 'show no partiality' in the life of faith (2:1). James's vocabulary itself is fascinating. Various scholars have suggested that perhaps he or his fellow Jewish Christians invented the word he uses to serve as a literal translation of the word picture embedded in the Hebrew term for partiality. It means 'to lift up or receive the face' of someone. Paul also uses it (in Rom. 2:11; Eph. 6:9; Col. 3:25). It conveys the idea of making discriminating judgements simply on the basis of outward appearances. The same root is used in connection with God himself—to underline that there is never any partiality in his character, attitudes, or actions. Did James have at the back of his mind the Lord's words to Samuel in connection with his choice of a king to replace Saul? 'The LORD sees not as man sees: man looks on the outward appearance, but the LORD looks on the heart' (1 Sam. 16:7).

So, we need to look beyond the clothes a person wears, the ring on their finger (be it a diamond engagement ring, a college ring—for that matter a Super-Bowl ring). And we need to look beyond the lack of them. Later in his letter James will provide the clue that helps us to do this: we are all made as the image and 'likeness of God' (3:9, cf. Gen. 1:26-28).

One senses a rising tide of sobering analysis of sin in what James goes on to say. Why is he so possessed of such righteous anger? Because he regards this kind of partiality as abhorrent to God.

SIN EXPOSED

It is all too characteristic of the sinful heart to excuse itself by appealing to extenuating circumstances—whether it be by claiming that we are not the only guilty parties or by saying that we are not gifted in dealing with 'people like that' (i.e. the humble or the poor!). Scripture's characteristic response is to put a name to our sin, to 'call a spade a spade'. We are guilty of distinctions—perhaps more bluntly put, we are guilty of discrimination—a form of sin that includes but is not limited to distinctions of race or colour.

James had already used this language in 1:6 of the divided or doubting heart. In such a person's life there is a deep spiritual instability. A deep-seated perversity in us needs to be exposed and put under the surgical scalpel if we are to be healed and go on to grow to spiritual maturity.

The amount of space James devotes to this issue suggests that he is not thinking merely hypothetically. He sees this as a clear and present danger, not only because of what it is in itself but because of what it says about us. In particular he unmasks two serious spiritual maladies in this kind of favouritism.

First, it means that I am blind to the attitude of God to the needy (2:5-6a). For God made provision for the poor in his law (Exod. 23:11; Deut. 15:7-11). Scripture is full of this. And not only the Old Testament, but also the New: 'He has filled the hungry with good things, and the rich he has sent away empty' (Luke 1:53); 'The Spirit of the Lord is upon me, because he has anointed me to proclaim good news to the poor' (Luke 4:18). This is the gospel of *grace*. To receive it we need to be brought to see our poverty (cf. Matt 5:3), to agree with the last words Martin Luther penned: 'We are beggars—this is true.' But these are precisely the ones who have become 'rich in faith and heirs of the kingdom' of God (James 2:5). James's half-brother said precisely this (Luke 6:20).

When the wonder of such grace to us in Christ dawns on us the spirit of favouritism is asphyxiated in us—it can no longer continue to breathe. We no longer assess people 'according to the flesh' (2 Cor. 5:16).

Think of Jonah in this context. He once showed favouritism to his own people and despised the pagan Ninevites—what did they deserve after all? They were not fit for the presence of God. But then, chastised, exposed for the proud prophet he was, he sees them through eyes cleansed by the tears of his own repentance and need of grace. Now he prays for those who 'forsake their hope of steadfast love' (Jon. 2:8).

Few things are more dangerous for a church than this attitude of favouritism becoming endemic in its life. For it is an evidence of satisfaction with our own reputation. And then the spirit of Laodicea sets in: 'People of this quality and standing come to churches like ours.' You say, 'I am rich, I have prospered, and I need nothing, not realizing that you are wretched, pitiable, poor, blind, and naked' (Rev. 3:17). That is why you dishonour the poor man (James 2:6). Notice that James does not say 'you have treated the poor man as a poor man'. Rather he exposes the true nature of the sin: 'you have dishonoured' him. He is in fact an heir of God and a joint heir with Christ (Rom. 8:16-17). He is highlighting the fact that this is not only inconsistent, it is sinful and shameful.

But second, if James's scattered correspondents were showing partiality to the rich and famous they were forgetting something: the attitude to the church which often characterizes rich people. He asks them three questions: Are not the rich (i) 'the ones who oppress you'? (ii) 'the ones who drag you into court?' (iii) 'the ones who blaspheme the honourable name by which you were called?' (2:6-7).

The form in which he expresses himself in Greek makes clear he expects the answer 'yes' to all three questions. By and large, James claims it is rich, not poor, people who exploit believers. They are the ones who wield influence and power. Rather than show mercy on the poor because of their needy circumstances, they drag them into court insisting all they want is what is theirs by right. It is the rich who flaunt their self-sufficiency, offend the heart of God (expressed in his law), and demean the name of Christ. What need have they of the Saviour of the humble poor?

How subtle is the thought 'If only we had more people of position and influence in our church, some famous people, media personalities, sports stars or the like, then we'd make an impact.' Of course, when that perspective has subliminally taken up lodging in our hearts and minds it will inevitably show itself in the false attitudes and dispositions against which James speaks here with such devastating force. For all this reveals is that our hearts have been invaded by the standpoint of the world, not of Christ. We are judging according to man and appearances, not according to God and reality.

Do you feel condemned? What is the answer?

DIVINE REMEDY

We all need to learn and relearn a basic principle in reading the Bible. We have seen that it rarely spells out answers to our 'How do you do that?' questions. We may therefore develop a tendency to think that we need to look elsewhere for them—perhaps a Christian book, or a conference or seminar? But in fact the answers are usually to be found by further meditation on the passage we are studying and its context. Paradoxically then, although people often speak about the practical emphases in the letter of James, sometimes he does not seem to give us a great deal of practical help! But look again, and we see that he does, both at the beginning and the end of the passage.

Over against the false disposition and lifestyle he has exposed and critiqued, he describes the lifestyle to which the gospel calls us.

He describes the privileges the gospel gives us. He reminds us of the new identity we have in Christ. The one in whom we have come to believe is both Lord and Christ. It is the Lord of glory to whom we now belong (2:1). Although he was rich he became poor with our poverty so that through his poverty we might become rich with his riches (2 Cor. 8:9). His is the 'honourable name by which [we] were called' (2:7).

James does not quite say this specifically, but clearly this is what it means to be baptized: to be called by the 'honourable name'.

Baptism is a naming ceremony: 'Go ... baptizing in [into] the name of the Father and of the Son and of the Holy Spirit' (Matt. 28:19). In it we receive a new name—the Lord's name. It is the sign of adoption into his family. There is no greater name in all the world—neither in heaven nor on earth—than that of Jesus Christ. And now he has given us his family name as it were. There is no greater dignity. And the marvel is this—whether we are wise or simple, old or young, male or female, and, yes, rich or poor—we have been dignified by the noble name of the Lord Jesus, not because of what we are but because of who he is and what he became for our sake. Our dignity and worth are found in him, not in ourselves.

When this dawns on us we say, 'From now on, therefore, we regard no one according to the flesh' (2 Cor. 5:16). We then cease to show favouritism because we realize what really matters: not wealth, possessions, background, position, or influence—but having the family name of Jesus Christ, which is given by grace, not because of anything that is to be found in any individual by nature.

Now we begin to see why showing partiality is so wrong. In fact, it undercuts the very foundations of the gospel. It is the antithesis of grace. For when we understand and respond to God's grace in Christ we say something like this:

When I was helpless, Christ died for me.
When I was poor, he enriched me.
When I was tainted by sin, he threw his arms around me.
When I was unloved, he kissed me in his grace.
When I was naked, he clothed me with his garments.
When I was an orphan, he brought me to his own Father.
When I had no friends, he gave me his whole family.
When earth left me starving, he fed me bread from heaven.
When nothing would satisfy my thirst, he gave me living water.
When I was in darkness, he gave me the light of life.
When I was lost, he found me.
When I was a stranger, he took me in.
When I was without hope, he gave me the hope of glory.
When I had nothing to give him, he gave me everything he had.
And when I die, he will let me live with him forever.

And once we realize this, we can never look at other people the way we once did, merely on the outside 'according to the flesh' (2 Cor.

5:16). For that would be unworthy of the 'honourable name by which you were called' (2:7). But there is a further consideration which is found towards the end of this passage (2:8-13). We are called to 'fulfil the royal law' (2:8) which is 'the law of liberty' (2:12, cf. 1:25). But what is this royal law?

James gives us a clue by quoting the words of Leviticus 19:18 which Jesus said constituted the second half of the greatest commandment (Deut. 6:5; Matt. 22:37). It is 'law' because Jesus our King has confirmed it. It is 'royal' because it describes the lifestyle of his kingdom.

The 'royal law' seems to be the Ten Commandments, expressed in their summary that we should 'love the Lord with all our heart … and our neighbour as ourselves' (Mark 12:30). Here James is speaking about our disposition towards others as a reflection of our understanding of our relationship to the Lord. This explains why he specifically cites commandments that reflect on 'love for neighbour', not directly on 'love for God'. If we fail in one part of the law we breach the whole (2:10), because we are sinning against the one who gave all the commandments.

But what are the interrelations in (i) not showing partiality, (ii) fulfilling the royal law, and (iii) becoming guilty of the whole law by failing in one point of it?

The connection in James's mind seems to have been as follows. Showing partiality is a breach of God's command to love our neighbour as ourselves. This in turn is the summary of all the commandments dealing with our relationships and dispositions to others. In essence it means to treat others in the light of the fact that they bear the image of God.

The lawyer who tested Jesus with the question 'Who is my neighbour?' was probably guilty of limiting 'neighbour' to people like himself, or the kind of person he aspired to be himself, and treating others with indifference. This is precisely what partiality does. And in effect it is saying, 'As far as I am concerned you would be just as good dead; you are certainly not worth my attention and care.'

Understanding the gospel and the law then provides us with motives that transform our thinking and thus gives impetus to the life of new obedience.

What then is the bottom line? How we act and speak (2:12-13). James had already written about the Christian's speech and he will do so again (3:1-12). The Christian is to remember that he or she is going to be judged by God on the basis of the law of liberty.

This law of liberty is not another, different law from the law of God, but that very law described in a way that emphasizes that we have received it in order to give structure to our Spirit-given freedom to love and serve the Lord. But it is standard as well as structure, and by it we will be judged, says James. And it carries with it this sobering implication: those who show no mercy, receive no mercy: 'judgement is without mercy to one who has shown no mercy' (2:13).

James is not falling back here on a principle of works righteous-ness (in exchange for mercy God will show mercy). No, he is simply echoing Jesus' teaching—not only from the Lord's Prayer (Matt. 6:12, 14-15), but in his parable of the servant whose massive debt his master forgave until he discovered that he had then tried under the most severe threats to extract the repayment of a comparatively trivial debt from a fellow servant (Matt. 18:21-35).

This is truly a sobering passage on what we sometimes superfi-cially imagine is a trivial sin—not showing mercy. How spiritually short-sighted we are if we assess it in the light of what others may be doing. We are like the man who looks in the mirror and sees a sinner saved entirely by God's sovereign mercy in Christ, and then goes away and lives in complete forgetfulness of what the mirror told him (1:23-24). How much more deeply the grace of God towards us in Christ needs to sink down into our thinking, our feeling, and into all our instinctive responses to others!

Living in obedience to the royal law leads to a nobility of life-style. Arthur Rendle Short (1880–1953) was a well-known evangel-ical Christian. He was Professor of Surgery at Bristol University and a Hunterian Professor of the Royal College of Surgeons (his brilliance was evident even as a student: he graduated with first class honours and Gold Medals in Physiology, Materia Medica, Anatomy, Medicine, Obstetrics—and also in Geology, meanwhile teaching himself Hebrew!). His son records the comments of one of his father's colleagues, not himself a Christian. He asked Short to examine a patient for him, and later commented to this effect: she was an old hag, filthy, smelly and disgusting. 'And yet Short treated her like a princess.'[1] This is the royal law of love for God and neighbour.

This is what the gospel of grace produces in someone who has been brought to 'hold the faith of our Lord Jesus Christ, the Lord of glory' (2:1). In his or her life 'mercy triumphs over judgement' (2:13). Here there is no spiritual racism in which partiality is shown to those who seem more important than others. No wonder James says that 'mercy triumphs'—that is, literally, *boasts*—'over judgement'! Partiality is defeated; mercy reigns!

But before we leave this section we should go back to its first sentence and to how James describes his half-brother as 'our Lord Jesus Christ, the Lord of glory'. These words rank with the descriptions of Jesus given by the one-time persecutor of the church, Saul of Tarsus. In some ways they are even more arresting, since Saul had a dramatic encounter with the risen Jesus. James, by contrast, was either an older or a younger brother of Jesus. They had lived in the same house, or presumably at least in the same community. He had seen Jesus at close quarters for years on end. Sometimes during Jesus' three years of public ministry James must have been an eyewitness. And of course, he knew Mary. It is one thing for a Jewish persecutor to become a follower of Jesus after a dramatic and clearly supernatural encounter with him and thereafter to call Jesus *kurios*; but in some ways it is even more remarkable and impressive that such a close relative as James would call him 'our Lord Jesus Christ, the Lord of glory'. After all, among his large family he would have been known simply as 'Jesus'.

If you ever doubt whether anyone who had known Jesus longer than three years really believed in his deity, remember James!

---

[1] John Rendle-Short, *The Green Eye of the Storm* (Edinburgh: Banner of Truth Trust, 1998), 108, 140.

6

Faith That Works

What good is it, my brothers, if someone says he has faith but does not have works? Can that faith save him? [15] If a brother or sister is poorly clothed and lacking in daily food, [16] and one of you says to them, 'Go in peace, be warmed and filled', without giving them the things needed for the body, what good is that? [17] So also faith by itself, if it does not have works, is dead.

[18] But someone will say, 'You have faith and I have works.' Show me your faith apart from your works, and I will show you my faith by my works. [19] You believe that God is one; you do well. Even the demons believe—and shudder! [20] Do you want to be shown, you foolish person, that faith apart from works is useless? [21] Was not Abraham our father justified by works when he offered up his son Isaac on the altar? [22] You see that faith was active along with his works, and faith was completed by his works; [23] and the Scripture was fulfilled that says, 'Abraham believed God, and it was counted to him as righteousness'—and he was called a friend of God. [24] You see that a person is justified by works and not by faith alone. [25] And in the same way was not also Rahab the prostitute justified by works when she received the messengers and sent them out by another way? [26] For as the body apart from the spirit is dead, so also faith apart from works is dead.

(James 2:14–26)

W ith James 2:14–26 a new section of the letter begins, or at least a new dimension in James's teaching on progress to spiritual maturity. It has also proved to be perhaps the most famous, and certainly the most controversial section in the entire letter.

Thus far we have traced the development of James's teaching in the following way:

In 1:4 he stated the theme he develops, namely how God brings our faith to maturity.

He then discussed how God does this.

First, he emphasized that the Lord does this by testing us. There are various kinds of tests, but they belong essentially to two categories: (i) The trials of life and (ii) The temptations we face.

Second, he emphasized that our growth to maturity is related to the way we respond to the word of God. Here he sees several false responses: (i) there is always the possibility of self-deception; (ii) there is the danger of favouritism. Now he moves on to a further dimension: (iii) the possibility of mere profession—professing faith that is not working faith is dead faith.

All this seems straightforward enough, until we come to his words in verse 24. It would be perfectly in order for any preacher to have them printed in the worship bulletin, or on the church website, as the title of this coming Sunday morning sermon: 'A person is justified by works and not by faith alone'. But if he did so, at least in some churches, he would be met by some very upset elders before he went into the pulpit! For is not this the very reverse of the gospel?

But these are the words of James, one of the authors of Scripture. Is it any wonder that in his Introduction to the New Testament (1522) Martin Luther called this 'a right strawy epistle' because he thought there was nothing of gospel in it?

Luther deserves some sympathy. He had dismantled the authority of the Roman Catholic Church. But until that point he had known what books should be counted as Scripture because the Church had told him. Now he had to begin again. What principle should he use? (What principle would you use if you had to start from scratch?). He decided that only books saturated with the gospel of justification by grace alone through faith alone apart from works should be treated as divinely given. It was a fair enough place to begin. But James 2:24 seemed to him to be a clear transgression of the principle—although in later editions of his Introduction he removed the offending sentence.

Yet James does say: 'You see that a person is justified by works and not by faith alone.'

It is very tempting, therefore, to treat these words as though they were the only important words in this passage—or even in the entire letter! There may even be book-browsers who, whenever they pick up a volume on the Letter of James, automatically turn to this particular section to discover 'What does he say about James 2:24? How does he reconcile James with Paul?'

But it is usually a mistake to approach any passage of Scripture with 'How can we solve the problem in this text?' as the first question in our minds. For the authors of Scripture did not write with the thought in mind 'How can I express myself in such a way that I will give my readers a problem to solve?'

So, before we rush in to ask how James and Paul are to be reconciled, we need first to listen to the text. It is, of course, possible that James had Paul's teaching in mind—or more accurately a perversion of that teaching which Paul was sometimes accused of holding (as he notes in Romans 3:8, 31). But in the absence of definite evidence, we should not simply assume that was the case. The best approach is to try to understand what James is saying within its context (think of what he had already written in 1:27), and in its own terms.

James begins with a question: Can faith without works be saving faith? 'What good is it … if someone says he has faith but does not have works? Can that faith save him?' He envisages a situation to illustrate his point: What good does it do to tell a fellow Christian who is poor and hungry, 'Peace be with you! May you be warm! May you be well fed!', without lifting a finger to clothe or feed them (2:15-16)? This kind of 'faith'—which James calls 'faith by itself'—which does not express itself in practical works—is dead. Perhaps the point would have been even clearer if our translations had paraphrased it 'faith-by-itself'. For clearly James does not mean that this person has *real* faith but with a small deficiency, namely, that it is 'by itself' (2:17). Rather he is beginning to prise apart two realities, both of which claim the same descriptor (*faith*) but are in fact two very different phenomena. And he states his thesis clearly in verse 17: 'faith-by-itself (i.e. which does not have works) is dead'.

He then explains this by an imagined conversation, almost a debate, in which he personifies these two realities as individuals. But he begins with what looks like an objection ('But someone will say,

"You have faith and I have works'", 2:18). James seems to envisage someone saying: 'I have my way—works; you have your way—faith. Both are valid!' 'No' says James: 'faith and works are inseparable! No works, then no faith. But also—no faith, no works!'

So, then, James is—

DRAWING A CONTRAST

The apparent complexity in James's argument is resolved when we realize he is contrasting two different people who both profess to be genuine believers. In fact, he sets up a debate between them in 2:15-26 (One person will say …; another person responds: 'Show me your faith … and I will show you').

If, in the style of John Bunyan, we give these protagonists names it may help us to follow James's reasoning. Let us call them 'A. Faith' and 'B. Faith'.

Imagine a school where the roll of a new class is being called out. The teacher calls out the name 'Faith'. Two voices respond, 'Present!' There are two students, Alex and Ben, who both have the name 'Faith'! The teacher decides to distinguish them now as 'A. Faith' and 'B. Faith'.

Think now of James. He imagines two people who both have the name of being 'believers'. He describes both as having faith; but he will eventually lead us to conclude that one of them is not really a believer at all. He has the name 'faith' but not its DNA. And the 'faith' he claims does not save.

Consider his description of 'A. Faith'. He has:

- Faith that does not have (or is apart from) works (2:14, 18, 20, 26).

That is to say, he has:

- Faith set in contrast to deeds (2:18)
- Faith by itself, i.e., unaccompanied by action (2:17)
- Faith alone, i.e., isolated from deeds (2:24)

But then consider how he describes 'B. Faith'. He has:

- Faith shown by its works (2:18).

That is to say, he has (like Abraham):

- Faith accompanied by actions (2:22)
- Faith consummated by actions (2:22)

James asks whether 'A. Faith' experiences salvation. The Greek language has the capacity to indicate the expected answer to a question by the way in which the question is asked. Here James uses the form which expects a negative answer. No, 'A. Faith' is not saved because his faith does not work.

What is the logic here? What is the presupposition that leads James to reach this conclusion? The only possible one is that saving faith always does work. Saving faith belongs only to 'B. Faith'. Unless professed faith is working faith, it is not saving faith and therefore cannot be true faith.

Sometimes students of Scripture coming to this passage on the assumption that the most important thing is to find a way of reconciling James to Paul have concluded that James uses the word *faith* in a different sense from Paul. But what we have discovered by taking the passage on its own terms is that James himself uses the word *faith* in two different senses.

REACHING A CONCLUSION

James not only speaks about saving and non-saving faith. What has created difficulties for many readers is that he also employs the language of *justification* and uses two different illustrations from the Old Testament (Abraham and Rahab) to prove his point.

At this point in the passage James hits his rhetorical stride in a major way. He tells 'A. Faith' that 'the demons' have as strong a faith as he has! They too can say the *Shema* ('Hear, O Israel: the LORD our God, the LORD is one', Deut. 6:4). Indeed, they 'shudder' at such a confession (2:19). And then he issues his bold challenge: 'Do you want to be shown, you foolish person, that faith apart from works is useless?' (2:20). We should recall Jesus' warning about calling anyone a 'fool' (Matt. 5:22) when we read what James writes here. He does not say this lightly.

This verges on extreme language on his part, stimulated by deep pastoral concern for the folly of 'A. Faith'. But James goes on to make an even bolder point, which he essentially repeats by means of two illustrations: 'Was not Abraham our father *justified by works* when he offered up his son Isaac on the altar?' (2:21; the incident, known as the *Akedah*, was one of the great moments in redemptive history and vividly recorded in Gen. 22:1-19). He will then confirm this principle by a similar appeal to the experience of 'Rahab the prostitute ... who was also *justified by works* when she received the messengers' (2:25; see Josh. 2:1-21). His conclusion? 'You see that a person is *justified by works* and not by faith alone' (2:24).

What are we to make of this? Does it seem to fly straight into the face of the apostle Paul? He taught us to 'hold that one is justified by faith *apart from works of the law*' (Rom. 3:28). He too used Abraham as an illustration; but it was to show that he was justified by faith, not by works (Rom. 4:1-3).

Once again, some students of Scripture have concluded that James must have been using the word *justify* in a different sense from Paul's usage.

But if we follow the development of James's reasoning this is an unnecessary approach to the text, and probably mistaken. For in verse 23 James cites the very same text as Paul does in Romans 4:3, namely Genesis 15:6.

Two considerations help us:

(i): The verb translated 'justify' (*dikaioō*) here, and throughout the New Testament, has a range of meanings, including 'to count or account someone or something as righteous/in the right; to vindicate'.

In some ways our standard English translation 'justify' can be misleading for two reasons:

(a) It is derived from the Latin *justificare*, a compound verb from *justus* (just, righteous) and the verb *facere*, to make—the verb used in the medieval church's Latin Bible. In a similar way the term *sanctification* is derived from *sanctus* (holy) and *facere*. But while sanctification is a work of God done to us and in us, justification is a declaration made about us.

(b) When we consistently translate the verb *dikaioō* as 'justify' we can easily mislead ourselves because we tend to attach a whole theology to the word, namely that the ungodly are justified by grace alone through faith alone. That creates a tendency to see every use of the verb through those lenses.

But clearly there are instances in the New Testament where *dikaioō* does not carry that theological freight and means simply 'to count as righteous'. Luke 7:29 and 35 provide examples. 'When all the people heard this, and the tax collectors too, they declared God just'; 'wisdom is justified by all her children'. In both instances the verb *dikaioō* is used. But it does not have the doctrinal overtones we associate with it. God is not 'justified' in the theological sense by tax collectors: he is not 'counted righteous by grace through faith'! Nor is personified wisdom 'counted righteous' in this sense either. Both are simply said to be what they actually are, namely 'righteous'.

Dikaioō can therefore mean (a) God counting sinners righteous in Christ, by grace, through faith, or (b) someone counting someone righteous because he does what is righteous.

If we keep this in mind it clarifies the connection between the key statements James makes. But we should not fail to notice the implicit recognition James gives here and elsewhere to the reliability and authority of the Scriptures by the way in which he appeals to them to settle the issue. For his whole argument assumes that if Scripture teaches something then it is true:

- Abraham was counted righteous when he offered up his son Isaac (2:21). He was counted righteous for doing this because it was a righteous thing to do—since God had told him to do it.

- But before this, Abraham was counted righteous when he believed God (2:23). Although he was a sinful man, he was counted righteous before God not because of what he had done to merit it but because he trusted in the Lord's promise of salvation in the promised seed (Rom. 4:1-5; Gen. 3:15; Gal. 3:15-18).

James himself explains the connection between these two statements as follows:

- faith was active along with his works (2:22)

and

- faith was completed by his works (2:22)

In other words: Abraham's work was accomplished because of

the faith that went along with it; and that work simply filled out (completed or fulfilled) his faith.

(ii) Put another way, what James is doing here is simply following through the story of Abraham. He does not see the statement of Genesis 15:6 (Paul's beloved text!), which rests justification instrumentally in faith, as contradicting the statement that 'Abraham was justified [i.e. considered righteous] by works [i.e. for what he did] when he offered up his son Isaac on the altar' (2:21; cf. Gen. 22:1-19). In fact, James says that not only did Abraham's willingness to sacrifice Isaac complete or fulfil the faith by which he trusted God's promise and was justified, but that the Scripture teaching in Genesis 15 was given a fulfilment in Genesis 22!

So, James makes quite clear that his double use of the verb *dikaioō* does not contradict Scripture but is consistent with it. He also shows us that the double counting of Abraham righteous is not contradictory but complementary. He who was already counted righteous by faith was later counted righteous because he was a justified man acting righteously! By faith he became rightly related to God in his covenant and was thus counted righteous; by his obedience he demonstrated it in a righteous deed, and for that he was counted righteous. In the first instance God counted the ungodly righteous by grace, in the second God counted the obedient righteous in life. As a sinner he was 'in the wrong' and God counted him 'in the right' through faith. As a justified saint he was 'in the right' when he offered up Isaac, and so (of course) he was counted 'in the right'.

James might well have been mystified by the later church's difficulties over what he wrote. Perhaps he would simply have said 'You are confusing the meaning of the verb with the use to which it is being put and reading into *dikaioō* your doctrine of justification by grace through faith in Christ.' But all that verb means is 'to account something/someone as righteous'; the ground on which that takes place is not part of the verb's basic meaning.

For good measure James then appeals to the example of Rahab to make the same point—as though to say: Notice that this is not true only for believers who come from the literal seed of Abraham, but for all, Jew and Gentile alike (2:25). Paul makes a similar point in Romans 4:9-12.

This perspective is by no means unique to James and his reading of the Abraham narrative. It is also true of David and his reading of his own life. He knew well the need for forgiveness (Psa. 32:1). But in two psalms he appeals to God on the basis of his own righteousness (Psa. 7:8; 18:20, 24). He is not implying that he can be justified based on his own works apart from grace (cf. Rom. 4:5-8); but he does appeal to God to be faithful to his covenant promises to him because he has been faithful to God. Later James will appeal to Elijah as an example of a righteous person (5:16-17), not in the sense that Elijah was justified by grace through faith (although he was!), but in the simple sense that (as a justified person) he acted in a way that was righteous.

The principle, then, is straightforward: *the person who is counted as righteous through faith will do what is righteous.* In that sense he or she is counted righteous (justified) by grace through faith, and as such is counted righteous (justified) because he or she lives righteously.

Would it not have been so much clearer (not to say far less controversial) for James to have reversed the order of verses 21-22 and verse 23, and written about Abraham in chronological order?

Perhaps; but we always need to be cautious in assuming we can make things clearer than the Holy Spirit has done! In fact, when we encounter passages like this in Scripture, where we might have expressed things differently, we should always ask if there might be a specific reason for the way the truth is expressed.

Ask that question here and the answer seems to lie on the surface. For notice what James accomplished. He has startled us a little, hasn't he? He even managed to irritate Martin Luther! This is exactly what he felt his readers needed. He is doing exactly what a pastor might do if he felt there was a tendency developing in his congregation to spiritual self-satisfaction, or a rising tide of interest in Bible study, or a new interest in studying doctrine—but no commensurate interest in practical Christian service. He might indeed use the words of verse 24 as his sermon title: '"*You see that a person is justified by works and not by faith alone*" ... *Or do you?*'

The key, then, lies in verse 18: 'I will show you my faith by my works.' What we do is the touchstone of faith. The faith that justifies is seen only by what a man does. The person who acts righteously is the man who is counted righteous (although he or she is not justified based on those acts). The person who has a deedless faith ('A. Faith') does not have true faith. He is not justified by a faith that does not express itself in righteous deeds. A false faith gives only a false salvation.

It is always worth remembering that we often use abstract terms to denote what are personal characteristics and actions. There is no such abstract entity as faith. It is not a commodity. Rather *faith is the New Testament's shorthand descriptive language for the person who knows, trusts in, and yields to Jesus Christ as Saviour and Lord.* In the very act of faith, he or she receives and rests on Christ alone, and yields himself or herself in obedience to him, saying 'Lord, what will you have me to do?'

We can put this another way. James is teaching us the following: if the 'I' who professes faith is not also an 'I' who obeys, then that 'I' does not truly believe with justifying faith.

The Westminster divines expressed this well, with an allusion to Galatians 5:6: 'Faith is the alone instrument of justification; yet it is never alone in the person justified, but is ever accompanied by all other saving graces, and is no dead faith, but worketh by love.'[1] Calvin says even more simply: 'Indeed, we confess with Paul that no other faith justifies "but faith working through love" (Gal. 5:6). But it does not take its power to justify from that working of love. Indeed, it justifies in no other way but in that it leads us into fellowship with the righteousness of Christ.'[2]

But perhaps it is Luther who expresses it most vividly: 'When it comes to faith, what a living, creative, active, powerful thing it is. It cannot do other than good at all times. It never waits to ask whether there is some good work to do. Rather, before the question is raised, it has done the deed, and keeps on doing it. A man not active in this way is a man without faith.'[3]

[1] *The Confession of Faith*, XI.ii.
[2] *Institutes of the Christian Religion*, tr. F. L. Battles, ed. J. T. McNeill (London: S.C.M. Press, 1960), III.xi.20.
[3] Martin Luther, 'Preface to the Epistle of St Paul to the Romans', in *The Reformation Writings of Martin Luther, volume II, The Spirit of the Reformation*, translated and edited by B. L. Woolf (London: Lutterworth Press, 1956), 288.

7

Guarding the Tongue

Not many of you should become teachers, my brothers, for you know that we who teach will be judged with greater strictness. ² For we all stumble in many ways. And if anyone does not stumble in what he says, he is a perfect man, able also to bridle his whole body. ³ If we put bits into the mouths of horses so that they obey us, we guide their whole bodies as well. ⁴ Look at the ships also: though they are so large and are driven by strong winds, they are guided by a very small rudder wherever the will of the pilot directs. ⁵ So also the tongue is a small member, yet it boasts of great things.

How great a forest is set ablaze by such a small fire! ⁶ And the tongue is a fire, a world of unrighteousness. The tongue is set among our members, staining the whole body, setting on fire the entire course of life, and set on fire by hell. ⁷ For every kind of beast and bird, of reptile and sea creature, can be tamed and has been tamed by mankind, ⁸ but no human being can tame the tongue. It is a restless evil, full of deadly poison. ⁹ With it we bless our Lord and Father, and with it we curse people who are made in the likeness of God. ¹⁰ From the same mouth come blessing and cursing. My brothers, these things ought not to be so. ¹¹ Does a spring pour forth from the same opening both fresh and salt water? ¹² Can a fig tree, my brothers, bear olives, or a grapevine produce figs? Neither can a salt pond yield fresh water.

(James 3:1-12)

W hat does it mean to be a well-developed, stable Christian? The Letter of James provides us with a working manual of practical Christianity to help us to grow to maturity. James has already taught us how this happens through the trials and temptations we experience and the way in which we respond to them, and also by God's living word doing its work in our lives.

James might have appreciated the witticism that we have been created with two ears but only one mouth for a reason. For he places tremendous emphasis on the way our hearing of God's word makes an impact on our use of the tongue. It does so because, in our spiritual anatomy, the tongue is directly connected to the heart and gives expression to it. The healthy Christian therefore will have a well-disciplined tongue.

James returns to this theme (already discussed in 1:19 and 1:26) at the beginning of chapter 3. But now it is more focused—on teachers (3:1). He warns us, 'Not many of you should become teachers.' The reason? Those 'who teach will be judged with greater strictness'.

Reading a New Testament letter is a little like listening in to a telephone conversation—we hear only half of it. Sometimes it is relatively easy to work out what the other side of the dialogue is. Other times we can only hazard a guess. Perhaps James is not only stating a fact but writing words of admonition: 'Be careful about your desire to be a teacher; you may be seeing only half the picture.'

Sometimes those who want to teach seem to be looking for position, or for gift-recognition, or for the opportunity to influence others, or even for reassurance that they matter. But the goal of a teacher in the church was never intended to be personal fulfilment and satisfaction—albeit those are often the side effects of the privilege. We must learn to think of teaching in a different way. It is a privilege, but it is also a responsibility because of the way it affects others. If we are given opportunities to teach then our service will be assessed on the 'Jesus principle' we have met before: 'as you did it to one of the least of these my brothers, you did it to me' (Matt. 25:40). Teaching is hard work; teaching God's word is very hard work. All who engage in it are to some extent under the charge Paul gave Timothy, 'I charge you in the presence of God and of Christ Jesus, who is to judge the living and the dead, and by his appearing and kingdom ...' (2 Tim. 4:1). To teach is to be exposed to the divine assessment.

If this is true, those who aspire to be teachers must make sure they do so out of pure motives. For a teacher must not only instruct in the truth but illustrate it in his life. He is called to be 'a perfect man'—that is a fully mature Christian—someone who does not 'stumble in what he says' and is 'able also to bridle his whole body' 3:2). There needs to be a harmony between what he teaches and how he teaches it by the way he lives.

James presses this point home in the words that follow. Whatever our gifts and aspirations may be, we must also remember that we are sinners: 'We all stumble in many ways' (3:2; notice the '*we*'—James includes himself).

Think of Isaiah, the most eloquent of all the Old Testament prophets. His oratory scales unsurpassed heights. But remember that he was first brought to acknowledge not only that he lived 'in the midst of a people of unclean lips' but that he was himself 'a man of unclean lips' (Isa. 6:5). Before we complain that our church does not recognize our gifts (a not unheard-of complaint!), we must first complain about ourselves and our sin—and realize that it weaves itself into our gifts not just our weaknesses. Remember, James cautions us, that if we are to be teachers we need to learn the mastery of the tongue. And that, in turn, requires the mastery of the whole body (3:2). For (as we saw in 1:19 and 1:26) what comes out of the mouth is a clue to what lies in the heart and affects the whole of our lives. The mature Christian is someone who can 'bridle his whole body' (3:2).

The use of this metaphor ('bridle') seems to set James's mind racing on in a flurry of imagery: bridles and horses, ships and rudders, winds and pilots, forests and fires, springs and water, fig trees and grapevines. But his basic argument develops simply in three sections (3:3-4; 5-8; 9-12):

DISPROPORTIONATE POWER

Two everyday illustrations help James to make the point that the significance and influence of the tongue is out of all proportion to its size.

Think of the control of his horse that was required for someone competing in a Roman chariot race. Or of a jockey in the Grand National or the Kentucky Derby. He controls his horse by means of a small bit placed in its mouth. Although it weighs no more than sixteen ounces, it enables the rider to control and harness the energy of a thoroughbred weighing perhaps a thousand to fifteen hundred pounds (or four hundred and fifty to seven hundred kilos) and travelling at over thirty-five miles per hour! The tongue is like that bit, writes James: small and light, but it harnesses the power of the whole person—for good or ill.

Again, the tongue is like the rudder of a ship. Rudders are much bigger and heavier than horse-bits, but then ships are much larger than horses. In proportion to the ship the rudder is small. And yet it can steer a great ship, driven by strong winds across the ocean. The person who controls the rudder is master of the whole vessel.

The tongue has no bone, but it can crush and destroy entire lives. Think of history's dictators and how they have swayed whole nations and brought so much conflict and death—by what? Yes, the use of the tongue. We should not be surprised, then, but rather deeply sobered, by Jesus' words: 'I tell you, on the day of judgement people will give account for every careless word they speak, for by your words you will be justified, and by your words you will be condemned' (Matt. 12:36-37). This is why the book of Proverbs is so densely packed with counsel about words and the use of the tongue (see for example, Prov.10:20; 12:18-19; 15:2, 4; 18:21; 21:23; 25:15).

The Christian who desires to teach must be mature to do two things with his tongue: (i) to speak words of life and encouragement that build others up (see, for example, Prov. 10:21), and (ii) to speak the truth in love (Eph. 4:15, 25), even if it hurts both hearer and speaker (and if it is going to hurt the former it should be sore for the latter too). And we are never fit to do the second until we can do the first.

Yes, 'the tongue is a small member, yet it boasts of great things' (3:5a).

DEVASTATING RESULTS

Now the metaphors continue as James gives us several more vivid word pictures. The tongue is like a fire (3:5b-6); it is an entire world (3:6); it stains everything (3:6); it acts like an untamed beast (3: 7-8); it is like a restless evil (3:8); it acts like a deadly poison (3:8). There is imagery here for a whole lifetime of self-examination—we need to take it all to heart.

The tongue can be dangerous. An entire forest can be set on fire by someone carelessly throwing away a lighted match.

Think of how quickly and uncontrollably fire spreads and how it takes lives in an instant. The tongue can be like that when it is set on fire by hell (3:6). It leads to setting on fire the entire course of life. It takes only a spark to produce an all-consuming blaze that can destroy a reputation, sully someone's entire ministry, or divide a church family. It can also produce slow-acting poison that debilitates others and may even damage their reputations for life. And if it is stimulated by the evil one it will participate in his restless evil. It will become uncontrollable—like Legion, always crying out, destructive of others and in the process destructive of self too (Mark 5:3-5).

Look at James's alarming conclusion: 'every kind of beast and bird, of reptile and sea creature, can be tamed and has been tamed by mankind, but no human being can tame the tongue' (3:7-8). It is amazing. Creatures great and small, gentle and wild, fast and slow, have all been tamed. But not the tongue! What is the evidence?

TRAGIC INCONSISTENCY

The evidence is found in the deep contradictions in what we say: we bless God, but we curse people made as his image. This is a contradiction not found in nature—not in fig trees, nor in grapevines, nor in salt ponds. They do not bear olives, or figs, or provide fresh water (3:11-12). The tongue acts in a manner unparalleled in the natural order of things.

Isaiah realized this and was utterly devastated by his discovery. Having pronounced six woes against others (Isa. 5:8, 11, 18, 20, 21, 22) he pronounced the final, climactic, seventh woe against himself! 'Woe is me! For I am lost; for I am a man of unclean lips …!' (Isa. 6:5).

Have we ever reached this conclusion about ourselves? If not, we are not yet ready to be teachers.

Notice that James says: 'My brothers, these things ought not to be so' (3:10). And while this is true universally (by definition what is sinful and evil ought not to be), it is particularly true for the Christian. But why?

It ought not to be because the first impact of the gospel brings about the exposure of our sinful hearts in order to cleanse and renew them—to silence boasting in ourselves so that we may boast only in the cross (Gal. 6:14).

This was also Paul's approach in Romans 1:18–3:20. Notice how he too has a focus on speech:

> None is righteous, no, not one ...
> Their *throat* is an open grave;
> They use their *tongues* to deceive.
> The venom of asps is under their *lips*.
> Their *mouth* is full of curses and bitterness (Rom. 3:10, 13-14).

What effect is this intended to have on us? 'Now we know that whatever the law says it speaks ... so that every *mouth* may be stopped, and the whole world may be held accountable to God' (Rom. 3:19).

Only the mouth that has been 'stopped'—as Isaiah's was—and then has felt the burning coal of forgiveness that comes from the curse-laden altar of the cross of Calvary—is fit to speak because it has been cleansed to speak well. This is the mouth that ceases to boast (3:5)—but will then be opened to boast in Christ (cf. Gal. 6:14).

But if this is so, James's words 'these things ought not to be so' (3:10) carry tremendous force for the Christian. How can he or she—of all people—bless God but then curse people who are made in the likeness of God (3:9)?

Do we? No wonder then if our speech leaves a bad taste. Non-Christians can spot it quickly.

Do you still love the Letter of James? It is surely obvious now how facile it is to say 'I love James because it is not so much theological but wonderfully practical.' That would be as naïve as saying 'I can't stand Paul and his theology, but I just love the Sermon on the Mount because it is so practical' (as many do who have never read it to the end or at least have never read it with any care).

Is James simply driving us to despair? Why does he offer no hope for us here? Was the younger Luther right, after all (despite what we have discovered in 2:14-26), that James is asking us to build bricks by giving us only straw?

We must not forget that the present passage is set within the broader context of the teaching James had already given. Otherwise we have once again become like the man who looks into the mirror (of the word) and then forgets what he was like (1:24). But when we consider the whole of James 1:1–3:12, we see that he is teaching us to go back to the mirror regularly, and to remember what we look like and who we are by God's grace. Retrace the steps then:

(i) Here in 3:1ff. James has exposed our sin, brought us to recognize it and to be deeply convicted of it. He has taught us the realistic, if unpalatable truth that no human being can tame the tongue (3:8).

(ii) In particular, he has shown us that un-Christlike speech ought not to be (3:10) because we have been given a new life in Christ. We are a kind of firstfruits of his creatures (1:18). New people develop new patterns and instincts in their lives. We need not despair. For Christ is not only 'a fountain opened … to cleanse … from sin and uncleanness' (Zech. 13:1), but also brings us to experience what Thomas Chalmers called 'the expulsive power of a new affection'—new instincts created in those who have been born again into the family of God. Like David, in whom God created a new heart, we now pray, 'O LORD, open my lips, and my mouth will declare your praise' (Psa. 51:15). That is the *sine qua non* for also being able to say, 'Then I will teach transgressors your ways, and sinners will return to you' (Psa. 51:13).

(iii) James has also taught us the importance of letting the word of God do its own work in our lives. Apostles, prophets, evangelists, pastors and teachers were all given to minister the word of God in order that we might put away falsehood and begin to 'speak the truth … Let no corrupting talk come out of your mouths, but only such as is good for building up, as fits the occasion, that it may give grace to those who hear … Let all bitterness and wrath and anger and clamour and slander be put away from you, along with all malice … Let there be no filthiness nor foolish talk nor crude joking, which are out of place, but instead let there be thanksgiving' (Eph. 4:25, 29, 31: 5:4). We learn to do this, and grow in these patterns of new life, when we follow the example of the Lord Jesus. First, he listened to the word of God, then he spoke:

The Lord God has given me
   the tongue of those who are taught,
that I may know how to sustain with a word
   him who is weary.
Morning by morning he awakens;
   he awakens my ear
   to hear as those who are taught.
The Lord God has opened my ear,
   and I was not rebellious (Isa. 50:4-5).

James is doing radical spiritual surgery here. But at the same time, he is teaching us to use our tongues to follow the perfect example of the one at whom people 'marvelled' because of 'the gracious words that were coming from his mouth' (Luke 4:22).

8

Showing Heavenly Wisdom

*Who is wise and understanding among you? By his good conduct
let him show his works in the meekness of wisdom. [14] But if you
have bitter jealousy and selfish ambition in your hearts, do not
boast and be false to the truth. [15] This is not the wisdom that
comes down from above, but is earthly, unspiritual, demonic.
[16] For where jealousy and selfish ambition exist, there will be
disorder and every vile practice. [17] But the wisdom from above
is first pure, then peaceable, gentle, open to reason, full of mercy
and good fruits, impartial and sincere. [18] And a harvest of
righteousness is sown in peace by those who make peace.*

(James 3:13-18)

James now turns to discuss the theme of *wisdom*. This will not
surprise us if we have followed him thus far, because there is so
much in his letter that reminds us of the wisdom books in the Old
Testament. Dealing with trials and temptations is a theme that is
present in the book of Job. Hearing and doing, speech and the use
of the tongue, overcoming temptation and negotiating trials are all
major themes in the book of Proverbs, which highlights the importance of wisdom (Prov. 1:2-7, 20-33; 2:1-15; 3:7, 13-14, 21-27, 35;
4:5-11; 5:1-6; 7:1-5; 8:1-31; 9:1-12; 10:1).

Wisdom depends on knowledge; but it is more than knowledge.
It involves knowing what to do with the knowledge we have and
understanding the best way to accomplish the goals God has given
us. It is not merely a '*what is*' kind of knowledge but also a '*how to*'
knowledge. This is why 'the meekness of wisdom' is revealed in
'good conduct' (3:13).

James contrasts the wisdom that is 'earthly' with the wisdom that is heavenly because it comes 'from above'—man's wisdom and God's wisdom. There is therefore not only 'A. Faith' and 'B. Faith'; there is also 'A. Wisdom' and 'B. Wisdom'!

TWO WISDOMS?

We should first notice here the different origins of these two wisdoms. It lay behind the great divide between human reason and divine revelation in antiquity. And it remains a key issue in the world today. It is worthwhile pausing here to see how relevant this contrast is to the present day, lest we think James is talking only about theoretical and abstract issues that have no bearing on our lives. To the contrary, it is a critical issue, theologically, practically and apologetically. It is vital we understand his antithesis.

Our culture is saturated with the wisdom that is 'earthly' (3:15). Its contemporary form can be traced back to the intellectual revolution we know as 'the Enlightenment'. Its effect was to convince people that we can have no certain knowledge of any transcendent reality—even if there is one.

Behind this lay what is often called 'the Cartesian Revolution'— reflecting the attempt of the philosopher-mathematician René Descartes (1596–1660) to find certainty and concluding that it was grounded in the self—hence his famous maxim *cogito ergo sum* ('I think, therefore I am'). This contrasted sharply with the biblical conviction which John Calvin laid as his starting point: 'Nearly all the wisdom we possess, that is to say true and sound wisdom, consists in the knowledge of God and of ourselves'.[1] Indeed, in every revision and expansion he completed of his great work, from 1536 to 1560, these opening words remained roughly the same.

But it is the Cartesian and Enlightenment perspective—the wisdom that comes from below—that has permeated the whole of our culture. One simple index of this is the abbreviation (and de-Christianization) of the mottoes of great universities. Harvard's original motto reflecting its Christian origins, *Veritas Christo et Ecclesiae* ('Truth for the sake of Christ and the Church') is now reduced to *Veritas*.

[1] Calvin, *Institutes*, I.i.1.

In contrast, the biblical conviction is that it is in Christ, the wisdom of God, that 'all things hold together' (Col. 1:17) because 'by him all things were created' (Col. 1:16), and therefore in him are 'hidden all the treasures of wisdom and knowledge' (Col. 2:3). This principle lies at the heart of the possibility of a *uni-versity*, and the possibility of there being a unified field of knowledge, because it lies at the heart of the uni-verse. Now, it is claimed, by contrast, that wisdom must be found below. James's teaching makes clear to us that such wisdom can never discover ultimate bedrock or effect an authentic unity either of knowledge or of the human race.

James's teaching on wisdom here follows on from his discussion of the use of the tongue. This in turn was set in the context of his warning to us not to over-hastily seek to be teachers because those who do teach will be judged with greater strictness (3:1). Some commentators think that this concern continues to run in the background through this section as well. If so the question 'Who is wise and understanding among you?' further explores the moral characteristics that are essential to those who are called to be teachers of God's people: 'By his good conduct let him show his works in the meekness of wisdom' (3:13).

But teachers are by no means the only Christians who need wisdom. While these words are especially applicable to them, and help to explain why those who teach will be judged with greater strictness (3:1), we all need wisdom.

RECOGNIZING TRUE WISDOM

We have seen that wisdom is more than education. One of the great fallacies of modernity is that all that is needed to solve the world's problems is more education. But often with more knowledge comes more sin. Learning how to use the worldwide web has brought many advantages, but it has also created a cosmos of cyber sin. By contrast, wisdom is not merely increased information. It is knowing what to do and how to live for the glory of God; the ability to use whatever knowledge we have, in whatever sphere we live, in a way that enables us to glorify and enjoy God, expressing his glory and our joy in very practical ways and in the practical details of our lives. That is why the book of Proverbs begins (in chapters 1 to 7) with what appears to be a series of father-son talks on the wise life followed by a further twenty-four chapters of practical illustrations of how wisdom works out in day-to-day life.

This explains the words 'By his good conduct let him [the wise person] show his good works in the meekness of wisdom.' Why 'meekness'? And how does it reveal itself in 'good conduct'?

Meekness should never be confused with weakness. Moses was the meekest man on earth (Num. 12:3); but he was far from being weak. Jesus described himself as meek (Matt. 11:29, translated *gentle*, ESV); but he was not a weak man. So, what is this meekness? It is yielding to the will of God in his word and being submissive to him in his providence. None of Moses' contemporaries had done that to the extent Moses did—for all his failings. Jesus did it perfectly. It is a leading characteristic of great Christian leaders; but it is always absent in false teachers. And it reveals itself in 'good conduct'.

This is a reliable and accurate translation. But probably the most frequent context in which we hear the expression 'good conduct' today is when a criminal has his prison sentence reduced 'for good conduct'. But here the adjective good (*kalos*) does not have the connotation of 'keeping the rules' but of being lovely, attractive, or beautiful. Think of the word 'calligraphy'—writing (*graphe*) that is aesthetically pleasing (*kalos*). James is thinking about the gracious, attractive bearing that conveys a sense of 'this is how life was meant to be lived'. Education, informational knowledge, does not produce that. It is produced only by a meek yielding to God's word, a humble submission to God's providence. It is reminiscent once more of Isaiah's portrait of the servant of the Lord:

> Morning by morning he awakens;
>   he awakens my ear
>   to hear as those who are taught.
> The Lord God has opened my ear,
>   and I was not rebellious;
>   I turned not backward.
> I gave my back to those who strike,
>   and my cheeks to those who pull out the beard;
> I hid not my face
>   from disgrace and spitting (Isa. 50:4-6).

These words came to a literal fulfilment in the one who described himself as 'meek'. He supremely and with deep sensitivity yielded both to God's word and to God's providence in his life.

TRUE WISDOM AND FALSE

But there is a false wisdom, even if it masquerades as the true. It is 'earthly, unspiritual, demonic' (3:15). Notice the intensification in James's description.

James describes both the fruit and the nature of this wisdom from below.

Its motivation is 'bitter jealousy and selfish ambition' (3:14). It is driven by narcissism, however thinly veiled. The project of 'the self' dominates everything, pursuing its own goals and harbouring grudges against those who have attained the goal before it manages to.

In turn, its fruit is twofold:

(i) It will 'boast'. It reveals itself in 'bitter jealousy and selfish ambition'. Of course, because what it lacks is 'meekness'. Never yielding to God's revealed will and his sovereign providence, Mr Worldly-Wiseman envies what someone else has but he lacks. He can never be content until he can boast in what he has achieved and what he possesses.

Almost inevitably therefore, worldly wisdom

(ii) will be 'false to the truth'. Since the truth of the gospel silences boasting, Mr Worldly-Wiseman must play fast and loose with that truth, even if he does so in subtle ways. He lacks 'the wisdom that comes down from above' that begins with 'the fear of the Lord' (Prov. 9:10)—that admiration of him and awe before him that means we want to live under his smile all of our lives, always pleasing him, never offending him.

James describes the nature of the wisdom that comes from below in three terse words in verse 15:

(i) It is 'earthly'. Paul uses the same adjective to describe the 'enemies of the cross' (Phil. 3:19). The wisdom of this world always sees time as long and eternity as short, man as big, God as small. It crucifies Jesus rather than worships him (Phil. 3:18, cf. 1 Cor. 1:21; 2:8). Inevitably, therefore, it clashes with 'the wisdom that comes down from above'.

(ii) It is 'unspiritual'. The word James uses here (*psuchikos*) means 'natural' in distinction from 'spiritual'. Human wisdom is dictated by concerns that leave no room for the work or will of the Spirit of God. The natural mind does not submit to God's law because the natural man cannot understand spiritual reality (Rom. 8:5-8; 1 Cor. 2:14).

(iii) But James adds a third description of this world's wisdom, and this is the most radical of all: it is 'demonic'. Of course. For if it is opposed to God's wisdom it belongs to an order of existence ruled over by the god of this age, 'the prince of the power of the air, the spirit that is now at work in the sons of disobedience—among whom we all once lived in the passions of our flesh …' (Eph. 2: 2-3). The world, after all, says the apostle of love, 'lies in the power of the evil one' (1 John 5:19).

The wisdom that comes from below is the false wisdom that was injected into the human race in the Garden of Eden. It is a refusal to take God's word as our authority, doubting his goodness as the foundation for our actions, and refusing his truth as the starting point for our interpretation of everything. All this leads to the acceptance of the evil one's lie that his interpretation of reality will bring true wisdom and true freedom from God.

But James is teaching us that to seek to be free from the wisdom of God is to be caught up in the vortex of this world's folly. For the wisdom that is found 'under the sun' (the phrase used almost thirty times by the author of Ecclesiastes to describe life seen from an exclusively this-world perspective) is no more successful than trying to catch the wind (Eccles. 2:17).

All this leads, as James has already indicated, to 'jealousy and selfish ambition' (3:16, cf. 3:14). It produces what the American cultural critic Christopher Lasch called 'the culture of narcissism'.

When the wisdom from below threw off the wisdom that comes down from above (as our Western culture has done progressively) it tended to assume society would return to its native basic goodness. This is the contemporary orthodoxy. Wisdom from below holds that people are 'basically good'. But the wisdom from above teaches us that this world's wisdom is false to the truth (3:14). It should not surprise us that when a culture dismantles the wisdom that comes from above it returns not to an imagined earlier decency but to a modernized form of what preceded the incoming of divine wisdom. That was, in fact, paganism: the worship of the creature and the creation, the rejection of God's revelation and the deconstruction of his creation ordinances. James is, in essence, stating the foundational principles that Paul would work out in greater detail in Romans 1:18-32. The result of exchanging the two wisdoms is inevitably 'disorder and every vile practice' (3:16). What was formerly regarded as 'disorder' becomes the new 'normal'; what was regarded as 'vile' is the new 'cool'. It is a transformation that has been witnessed in the contemporary world.

To thus become 'false to the truth' (3:14) is not a relatively harmless marginal deviation from the divine norm. It means that we no longer see things as they really are. Here again James is in harmony with Paul: we claim to be wise, but we have actually become fools (Rom. 1:22). Thus, governments and societies pursue and promote policies that are self-destructive and systematically resist the wisdom that comes down from above. They are committed, usually without acknowledging it, to the superiority of their wisdom to the wisdom of the Creator.

The unwisdom of this exchange appears in cultures that remove God's basic order from the fundamental syllabus of life (summarized, remarkably, in only ten commandments!). The result is a proliferation of new laws required to restrain the effects of the abandonment of God's law. It should not surprise us that idolizing the wisdom that comes from below has led to a massive loss in the sense of identity and purpose of so many young people. Disorder has become the new order of the day.

James by contrast understood (with the wise John Newton long after him) that 'Solid joys and lasting treasures [and pleasures too!] none but Zion's children know.'[1]

This leads to the obvious question: *What then is true wisdom like and how do we get it?* James does not leave each of us to find his or her own personal answer to that question.

CULTIVATING TRUE WISDOM

In verses 17 and 18, James hints at how we are to develop wisdom and also describes what it looks like in the daily lifestyle of a Christian believer.

True wisdom is 'from above' (3:17). But where do we find it? Once again, James has already hinted at his answers.

First, remember he described Jesus as 'the Lord of glory' (2:1). By definition he is the one who has come from above (i.e. from that

---

[1] From the hymn 'Glorious things of thee are spoken' by John Newton (1725–1807).

glory). True wisdom is therefore to be found in Christ. He is 'the wisdom of God' (1 Cor. 1:24); 'all the treasures of wisdom' are found in him (Col. 2:3), and he 'became to us wisdom from God' (1 Cor. 1:30). We gain wisdom by watching him, by meditating on how he thought and lived, by growing in appreciation of his salvation, and by following his example.

Second, James has emphasized that everything that is good also comes from above (1:17). So, wisdom involves believing that God himself is good, that everything he does for us is for our good, and that all his directives for our lives are both good in themselves and good for us.

Third, the depository in which we will learn wisdom from above is the Scriptures God has given to us. As we 'receive with meekness the implanted word' (1:21) we will discover how it is able to make us 'wise for salvation' (2 Tim. 3:15; cf. Psa. 119:18).

Fourth, we will grow in our understanding and in our ability to live wisely as we live in God's presence and ask him to give us wisdom: 'If any of you lacks wisdom, let him ask God, who gives generously to all without reproach, and it will be given him' (1:5).

What then will such wisdom produce in our lives? In verses 17 and 18, the floodgates seem to open in James's mind. A river of descriptions flows on, each one highlighting the difference wisdom makes to our lives: pure, peaceable, gentle, open to reason, full of mercy and good fruits, impartial and sincere.

These words are somewhat reminiscent of the beatitudes with which Jesus began the Sermon on the Mount (Matt. 5:1-12). It is as though James is subliminally reminding us that however counter-cultural the Christian life may seem to be it is Christ's way and therefore the way of blessedness. At the same time, these verses remind us of Paul's description of love in 1 Corinthians 13. The life of genuine love is directed by divine wisdom and it alone leads to divine blessing. But more than this, James's words remind us, most of all, of his half-brother, 'our Lord Jesus Christ, the Lord of glory' (2:1).

WISDOM DESCRIBED

Wisdom is 'pure'. It is the pure in heart who see God (Matt. 5:8).

This is the goal of the wise person. He or she realizes that God is holy. The desire to see God has an inevitable corollary. It makes us want to be like him and to reflect his purity.

This is blessedness. It is also simple logic. But it flies in the face of the wisdom from below that regards purity as outmoded. In addition it sees the call to purity as an objectionable restraint on our right to decide how we will live. Austerity indeed! But notice that what the world counts as moral 'austerity' James, like Jesus, sees as blessedness (Matt. 5:8).

This is such an important principle to grasp right at the start of the Christian life. No Christian was ever made miserable by purity; many (not least King David) have been made miserable by neglecting it.

Wisdom is also 'peaceable'. Once more we are reminded of the beatitudes. The servants of the Prince of Peace enjoy peace with God and are peacemakers. A new *shalom* lies at the heart of their lives. Reconciled to God in Christ they desire to 'live peaceably with all' (Rom. 12:18). Christians do not chase after peace at any price. But they do make sure that the peace of Christ rules in their hearts (Col. 3:15). They do not do this in the sense that we sometimes hear ('I feel a peace about it, so it must be right'); but rather by acknowledging Christ's peace as the ruling principle of their actions and aspirations, especially in the church family. There, 'in one body', peace acts like an umpire or a referee (Col. 3:15; Paul's verb *brabeuō* means to act as a judge, or to award prizes in a contest). This, then, is one of the principles on the basis of which we act or speak: *Will this promote the peace of Christ?*

In addition, wisdom is 'gentle'. This too is a Christlike grace. Paul appealed to the wayward Corinthians on the basis of the 'gentleness of Christ' (2 Cor. 10:1). This explains why wisdom is also peaceable. Yes, there are times when firm speech or action is required. But there are also occasions when 'a soft answer turns away wrath' (Prov. 15:1), and even occasions when 'with patience a ruler may be persuaded, and a soft tongue will break a bone' (Prov. 25:15).

Wisdom is, therefore, 'open to reason'. The wise Christian develops the habit of weighing up both sides of an argument. This is why he or she becomes 'quick to hear, slow to speak, slow to anger' (1:19)—especially in the context of a disagreement. Christians are to be characterized by 'sweet reasonableness' (cf. Phil. 4:5). This contrasts sharply with the argumentativeness that harms relationships, destroys marriages and homes, and sometimes churches too.

Mark tells us how Jesus himself exemplified this trait. A Syrophoenician woman asked him to exorcize her daughter. Jesus tested her faith—as he often did with people—by replying that he had been sent to his own people. His words were perhaps simply a proverbial expression: 'It is not right to take the children's bread and throw it to the dogs.' But the woman replies with logic born of faith: 'Yes, Lord; yet even the dogs under the table eat the children's crumbs.' She reasons with Jesus; and Jesus is open to reason! The truth is, he loves to be reasoned with! In this way he brings us to the heart of the matter (cf. Mark 7:24-30).

This is what being open to reason means. It is an indication we want to get to the heart of the matter.

As a result, wisdom is also 'full of mercy and good fruits'. Think of it this way. Someone is in need. You say to them, 'If there is anything I can do for you, let me know.' That may seem to be a kind offer, but it lacks wisdom. For wisdom sees what needs to be done and finds ways of providing practical help and succour. This was the wisdom of the Good Samaritan. The priest and the Levite could hardly avoid seeing the needs of the man who had been the victim of robbers. But the Samaritan not only saw the need and felt for the man; he saw what to do about it (Luke 10:25-37). That is wisdom. And when it is full of mercy it also realizes that this is only the beginning, for all good fruits—that is the fruit of the Spirit—will then be released to minister to others.

Moreover, in all this, wisdom will be 'impartial'. It can afford to be so because it is set free from the selfish distortion that marks the wisdom that comes from below. It can respond to each individual appropriately because it understands the basic biblical truths that

(i) we are all created as the image of God (Gen. 1:26-28; cf. James 3:9);

(ii) we have all sinned and fall short of God's glory (Rom. 3:23);

(iii) Christ 'is able to save to the uttermost those who draw near to God through him' (Heb. 7:25) .

Finally, James says, wisdom that comes down from above is 'sincere'. The English *sincere* and the Greek it translates (*anupokritos*) are picture words. One possible derivation of sincere is from the

Latin *sine* (without) and *cera* (wax). If so, the background picture is of a damaged work of art (a bust of Caesar, for example) being repaired by filling in the damage with wax and then covering it. Sincere—without wax—implies integrity, being the genuine article, not having artificial filler as it were. The Greek word has a more definite background. The word *hupokritēs* means an actor. In the theatres of antiquity, the actors wore masks—they did not spend long hours in 'make up'. Thus *anupokritēs* means that the Christian is not an actor who is one thing in his personal and private life, but another on the stage.

Christians are people whose masks have been torn off by the word of God; they have faced the terrible truth about themselves as sinners; they have been accepted by God in Christ. They no longer need to pretend to him, and so they no longer find it necessary or important to pretend to others—either that they are something they are not, or not something they are. The wisdom from above sets them free from the tyranny imposed on them by living for themselves and following the wisdom that comes from below.

This is why, at the end of the day, the lives of the wise bear such rich fruit, for 'a harvest of righteousness is sown in peace by those who make peace' (3:18). Peace seems a very modest grace indeed, very down-to-earth, very day-to-day, very unspectacular. But it is a seed that issues in a great harvest. Peace creates righteousness.

Only when you have found Christ, who is Wisdom, do you gain the wisdom to care for his glory, to enjoy his grace, to be delivered from self and the need to wear a mask. And only then can you experience and spread the peace of God.

While this is not a long section in the Letter of James, it is very detailed. And before we leave its details we should return to the question with which James began (3:13), and ask it of ourselves and our church family:

> Who is wise and understanding among you? By his good conduct
> let him show his works in the meekness of wisdom.

[79]

9

Avoiding Worldliness

What causes quarrels and what causes fights among you? Is it not this, that your passions are at war within you? ² *You desire and do not have, so you murder. You covet and cannot obtain, so you fight and quarrel. You do not have, because you do not ask.* ³ *You ask and do not receive, because you ask wrongly, to spend it on your passions.* ⁴ *You adulterous people! Do you not know that friendship with the world is enmity with God? Therefore whoever wishes to be a friend of the world makes himself an enemy of God.* ⁵ *Or do you suppose it is to no purpose that the Scripture says, 'He yearns jealously over the spirit that he has made to dwell in us'?* ⁶ *But he gives more grace. Therefore it says, 'God opposes the proud, but gives grace to the humble.'*

(James 4:1-6)

When you make an appointment to see your physician you go in hope. You hope that there is nothing wrong, or at least hope that it is not serious. You certainly hope that your doctor can diagnose the problem. Most of all, you hope that if there is a problem then there will also be a prescription, or at worst an operation, that can help you. Sometimes however your physician will make an appointment for you to see another doctor, someone with the appropriate experience, and the necessary diagnostic or surgical skills, to help you. Perhaps the first readers of this little letter of James were in a similar position spiritually. They were scattered (1:1). They probably met in small numbers in different places. We know that they had 'elders' (5:14). James was presumably not intending to usurp their ministry. But perhaps they were all conscious that they needed help from outside—someone with greater diagnostic skills than they themselves possessed. They needed Dr James who had been such a help to them in the past!

Dr James is nothing if not thorough, and he is realistic; he is also a serious spiritual clinician and gets to the point. Watching him at work here is like being taken into the office of a master physician of the soul. He now puts his finger on the problem.

SYMPTOMS

Do Christians have 'quarrels' and 'fights'? 'Quarrels' probably refers to an entrenched spirit while 'fights' perhaps describes specific flare-ups, outbreaks of sharp disagreement. But is James talking about the church?

Our reaction to James's statement reveals a great deal about ourselves, our view of our church, and indeed our understanding of the gospel. For we can be as much 'in denial' about the health of the body of Christ to which we belong as we sometimes are about our own bodies: 'I am sure it is nothing to bother about … just an occasional pain … I am feeling quite well otherwise, thank you … I wasn't sure it was even serious enough to bother you about … .' But the shrewd physician wants to examine us; he takes note of what we say, but he wants to use his hands, his eyes and his ears—to touch, see, and hear what our body tells him. He will not be content with our self-protective diagnosis!

Here are two church members. Their relatively new pastor is puzzled by something he has noticed in the attitude of one of them until he is told 'they have been at war with each other for the past twenty years'. What the pastor has noticed was a subtle clue to hostilities in an ongoing but largely hidden quarrel.

How do we react?

It is not unusual for Christians to say: 'That kind of thing does not happen in a church like ours.' But James does not make that mistake. He knew it happened in churches like his! Notice the words 'among you' in verse 1. He is simply noting the symptoms of disorder he sees among his fellow Christians—people for whom he has a pastoral responsibility. Yes, even people who could say, 'You know, I used to have James, the brother of our Lord, as my pastor' were capable of behaving in an ungodly way.

'Get them to stop!' That is a typical response to such situations in the church. But James knows that stopping the spread of infection requires getting to the source of the problem. He wants to know the cause before he prescribes the cure. Hence his first question is: 'What causes ...?' The answer is 'your passions are at war within you' (4:1).

The word 'passions' has the basic meaning of pleasures (the Greek noun is *hēdonē*, from which the English word 'hedonism' is derived). Here, clearly, there is an unpleasant odour attached to the idea. It refers to the spirit of putting your own pleasure—what satisfies your own senses—above every other consideration. It is the insistence on 'my way' which in turn is a dangerous symptom of a not-too-well disguised narcissism, a love of self that is the antithesis of the love of God. It will always, eventually, produce dissension. If we fail to win the war within we will not ever see the 'harvest of righteousness ... sown in peace by those who make peace' to which James referred in the previous verse (3:18—we should remember that James himself did not think of that as the closing statement of James chapter 3!).

But Dr James has only just begun. He now initiates a closer examination—like a physician sending a culture to the pathology laboratory for analysis.

PATHOLOGY REPORT

Most of us are familiar today with medical or crime dramas on television in which we (the viewers) are initiated into the wonders of scientific analysis—even if we are somewhat amused by the technique of explaining the intricacies to the viewer by members of the team, or squad, all contributing information to each other about what they are doing!

So, what does James discover?

Notice what is on the spiritual pathology laboratory report. He lists four dominant features:

1. *Desiring but not having, leading to murder* (4:2). The idea here seems to be that if we do not (always) get what we want then we will take it by force. But 'murder'? Perhaps there is some unmentioned context of which James is thinking, one to which we have no access. Perhaps—as in 1:14-15—the story of David and Bathsheba

is still playing in the background of his thinking? Or perhaps he is reflecting on Jesus' teaching that it is possible to kill with words as well as with knives (Matt. 5: 21-22).

One thing leads to another. That is a lesson we need to learn repeatedly. This pathology report is important for us for many reasons; one of them is to alert us to how sin works, to help us to see that the seed of desire may bring forth the fruit of death.

2. *Coveting, but not obtaining, leading to fights and quarrels* (4:2). If desiring refers to warped desires, then to covet is simply the next step. We want what someone else has, and by implication we do not want them to have it. If we do not get it, what is the result? Often in a roundabout fashion, we find ways of disagreeing with the person who has what we covet; that leads to criticism of them, which in turn leads us to fight and then to quarrel. The real issues lie hidden in the deep recesses of our hearts. But the pathology report gets to the bottom of things. James's spiritual microscope reveals what has been disguised: 'covetousness, which is idolatry' (Col. 3:5).

3. *Not having because not asking* (4:2). Here is an insightful diagnosis: coveting is a fruit of desiring but not having; but this develops out of a life of prayerlessness. Again, there is an echo of Jesus' teaching here, or to be more precise an understanding of what it implied: 'ask, and it will be given to you; seek, and you will find; knock, and it will be opened to you. For everyone who asks receives, and the one who seeks finds, and to the one who knocks it will be opened' (Luke 11:9-10). God gives us what we need; he wants us to know that what we need he provides, and therefore he often makes giving it to us dependent on our asking.

There is a shrewd understanding of the human heart here. For why did you not ask? Was it because you knew in your heart that you did not need, and therefore knew you could not go open-hearted and open-handed to the Father who gives 'every good gift and every perfect gift' (1:17)? And so, you behaved like Eve in the Garden of Eden—if God will not give it to you, you will take it yourself. And then you discover that what you have taken for yourself is not what you really needed.

4. *Not receiving because asking wrongly, in order to satisfy our personal passions* (4:3). You did ask; but your motives were not merely somewhat mixed (we are always still sinful even when we pray);

they were carnal and self-obsessed. We do not so much *pray* to God, but *prey* upon God. We ask in the wrong way and with the wrong motives ('you ask wrongly, to spend it on your passions', 4:3). And the result? Instead of repenting, that is acknowledging our sin and blaming ourselves, we resent not having what others have. 'Why should they get what they want? Why do they get their way when I don't get my way?'

If this is what comes back on our spiritual pathology report, is it any wonder there are 'quarrels and ... fights' in our church?

So, when James raises his eyes from the pathology report to the patient we can see that he has some very serious news indeed.

DIAGNOSIS

'What is it, Doctor? Do you have a diagnosis?' we ask. James is not smiling now. One devastating word crosses his lips slowly. It takes us totally by surprise: 'Adultery' (4:4)!

It is not what we expected. But remember how deeply the story of how David fell to temptation and sin seems to have imprinted itself on the way he sees things. There is no point in saying, 'But I have never broken the seventh commandment!' James is like one of the Old Testament prophets who used the marriage covenant as a parable of our relationship to God (e.g. Jer. 31:32; Ezek. 16:8). He sees the scarlet letter 'A' in our soul.

'Friendship with the world' leads to adultery in our relation-ship with God, indeed to what James calls 'enmity with God' (4:4). How does this happen? What are the tell-tale signs leading to adultery?

Often the marriage relationship has become jaded, and at the same time our real commitment level is exposed for its lack of depth and resilience. Feelings trump discipline. Our immune system is low. We become prone to the attractions and attractiveness of someone else. We begin to prefer to spend time with them; we find their com-pany more 'stimulating'; one thing leads to another; the friendship develops, and then we commit adultery. It may happen in a matter of hours, or it may take months. But in the process an enmity towards our spouse is built up—whatever pretence is made. The fatuous expression 'I still love her, but I am no longer "in love" with her' confuses emotional conditions with personal commitment. How can it be that two people who committed themselves to spending the rest of their lives together can no longer tolerate living in the same house? Promised love has turned into enmity. That is an echo of our spiritual adultery—'Although I still love God, this other love is important to me. I must have it.' But the truth will emerge in the entail. I can no longer live in the same home as God; enmity will build up against him, and he will become, ultimately, my enemy.

Apparently it is possible to deceive ourselves (1 Cor. 3:18; 2 Tim 3:13; 1 John 1:8). But James has a name for what has happened in our hearts: *adultery*. And its symptom? We prefer 'friendship with the world' to friendship with God. And we do not seem to realize that this is enmity with God (4:4).

Dr James leans over toward us and says very carefully: 'You have a choice to make, my friend: Do you not know that friendship with the world is enmity with God? Therefore whoever wishes to be a friend of the world makes himself an enemy of God. Or do you suppose it is to no purpose that the Scripture says, "He yearns jealously over the spirit that he has made to dwell in us"?' (4:4b-5).

So, we perhaps should engage in serious self-examination. Are there activities I much prefer to spending time with the Lord? Am I more at home, more comfortable, with worldly people than I am with godly people? Is there something of the Demas-spirit growing in me so that I am developing an attraction for 'this present world' that is greater than my love for Christ's appearing (2 Tim. 4:10, cf. 2 Tim. 4:8)? It all begins with a mild flirtation. But one thing leads to another ...

Is there any hope for us?

PROGNOSIS AND HOPE

Is a cure possible? Yes indeed; but Dr James insists that we must take the medicine and complete the course of treatment he prescribes; nothing else will cure us.

As a good physician, James takes us back to first principles. Before he explains the nature of the medicine and how to take it—what God provides for us and how we are to respond to it—he tells us something about God himself and the perspective he has on our lives. He thus provides both a foundation and motivation for taking the medicine and believing it will help us.

There is a general as well as a specific principle to note here.

The general principle is this: all spiritual dysfunction can be, and indeed should be, traced back to an inaccurate, false, or distorted view of God—in a word, to bad theology. Here again James gives the lie to the popular notion that his letter is full of practical applications rather than doctrine. Doctrine drives his teaching just as clearly as a physician's knowledge of human anatomy and physiology drives his or her approach to healing.

But it is the specific focus of this principle that is so arresting here. What have we forgotten when we make the world our friend? James states it plainly: God is a jealous God: 'do you suppose it is to no purpose that the Scripture says, "He yearns jealously over the spirit that he has made to dwell in us"' (4:5).[1]

There is a false and sinful jealousy which is condemned in Scripture. It is an uncontrolled interest in ourselves, and envy of what others possess but we lack. James had already exposed that kind of jealousy in verse 2. But the jealousy of God is different. It is his proper zeal to possess what rightly belongs to him. It is the jealousy that only true and pure love knows: to possess the loved one entirely and to do so for their good and blessing. This is the jealousy the Lord attributes to himself (in such passages as Exod. 20:5; 34:14).

It is within the context of this covenant love for his people that Moses declares 'The LORD your God is a consuming fire, a jealous God ... the LORD your God is a merciful God. He will not leave you or destroy you or forget the covenant with your fathers that he swore to them' (Deut. 4:24, 31). This is the pure love of the only devotion to us that can bless us through time and eternity. It must, in its very nature, be willing to consume anything that prevents that blessing being enjoyed by the object of its love. There is no price God will not pay to have all of us. We should have learned that from the cross (Rom. 8:32). His is a love that led him to see his Son experience sin-and-judgement bearing God-forsakenness on our behalf. To be 'a friend of the world' in the face of such love is to show we have not begun to understand the nature of the gospel and therefore we have little sense of who God really is.

---

[1] These words are not a quotation from any specific verse in the Old Testament, but a summary of its teaching. The quotation marks may be slightly misleading.

James's words are necessary and sobering in equal measure. We might think that he is giving us no hope. But experienced physicians can see the possibility of recovery when relatives see only ongoing weakness.

So now James issues his prognosis. He is not yet disclosing the course of treatment we will need to follow. Rather he is stating for us the principle on which such treatment will work. It is threefold: (i) God gives more grace; (ii) God resists the proud; (iii) God exalts the humble (4:6). His words are cited from Proverbs 3:34 in the ancient Greek version of the Old Testament (the *Septuagint*). The gospel tells us what we need to hear: there is greater grace in God than there is sin in us. Where sin abounded in history, grace has superabounded in Jesus Christ (cf. Rom. 5:20). But grace is resisted by the proud and therefore God resists them. Yet when sinners come to Christ they are able to say, 'from his fullness we have all received, grace upon grace' (John 1:16).

So, if we are ready to become humble, there is a real hope of our restoration to a life of friendship with God.

> O Jesus, full of pardoning grace,
>   More full of grace than I of sin,
> Yet once again I seek thy face,
>   Open thine arms and take me in
> And freely my backslidings heal
> And love the faithless sinner still.[1]

---

[1] From the hymn by Charles Wesley (1707-88), 'O Jesus, full of pardoning grace'.

10

Expressing Repentance

But he gives more grace. Therefore it says, 'God opposes the proud, but gives grace to the humble.' ⁷ Submit yourselves therefore to God. Resist the devil, and he will flee from you. ⁸ Draw near to God, and he will draw near to you. Cleanse your hands, you sinners, and purify your hearts, you double-minded. ⁹ Be wretched and mourn and weep. Let your laughter be turned to mourning and your joy to gloom. ¹⁰ Humble yourselves before the Lord, and he will exalt you.

¹¹ Do not speak evil against one another, brothers. The one who speaks against a brother or judges his brother, speaks evil against the law and judges the law. But if you judge the law, you are not a doer of the law but a judge. ¹² There is only one lawgiver and judge, he who is able to save and to destroy. But who are you to judge your neighbour?

(James 4:6-12)

James is concerned about the spiritual health of his correspond-ents. He is a skilled spiritual physician. He examines the symp-toms, engages in a spiritual analysis, comes to a diagnosis, and then gives us his prescription and prognosis. Since all spiritual ills stem ultimately from a wrong view of God, or a wrong response to him, he sits us down, looks us in the eye, and says: 'If you are going to be restored to health and strength you need to understand this: God is a jealous God: he has poured himself out in love for you in the gift of his Son on the cross and the gift of his Spirit sent into your heart. You are only going to make real progress towards a healthy Christian life if you let that sink in, absorb its implications and allow it to shape your mind, your will and your affections.'

Sometimes the connecting words in the New Testament letters are very illuminating. They make it clear how and why one thought logically leads to another (think of the number of times 'therefore' is used in Paul's letters). But sometimes they can be quite puzzling. Why, for example, does verse 6 begin with '*But* he gives more grace' and continue with 'Submit *therefore*'? Why '*but*' and '*therefore*'?

Perhaps it is the deeply solemnizing tone of his diagnosis that explains James's use of an adversative conjunction ('but' in 4:6). Is he now saying something like this? 'Do not draw the wrong conclusion from God's jealousy and shrink back from him. Yes, there is a sense in which the sheer intensity of his love for you is almost frightening, because he will not rest content until he possesses all of you. But remember, this is the God of grace who is jealous, the one who has given his Son for you! No matter how deep your sin may be, his grace is deeper still.'

What then is the logic that leads from verse 6a ('God gives more grace') to verse 6b ('*Therefore* it says, "God opposes the proud but gives grace to the humble"')?[1]

Notice in passing the way James refers to the Scriptures: 'it says'. He clearly sees them as the final authority that settles the issue. For the authors of the New Testament 'It says', 'Scripture says', and 'God says' are synonymous expressions.[2]

James' fundamental concern here is to cite Scripture as his authority for saying that God gives more grace. But at the same time he uses a text from the Old Testament that prevents us from thinking that receiving God's grace allows us to be indifferent to our sin. For the grace-giving God is also the pride-resisting God. Indeed, humility is necessary if we are to be willing to take the prescribed medicine. There is no room for pride here. We are in a recovery programme as sinners who need to humble ourselves under God's mighty hand if we are to be lifted up again at the proper time (1 Pet. 5:6—words Peter dictated immediately after citing this same text from Proverbs 3:34; in turn, James echoes Peter's words in 4:10).

[1] The words are quoted from Prov. 3:34 in the *Septuagint* (the Greek translation of the Hebrew Bible used throughout the Roman Empire).

[2] For a full exposition of this and its implications see '"It Says"; "Scripture Says"; "God Says"' in B. B. Warfield, *Revelation and Inspiration* (New York: Oxford University Press, 1927), 283-332.

What is the health-producing regimen that James prescribes? It is a multi-dimensional programme for recovering sinners. It is what the rest of Scripture calls 'repentance'. Just as the medical doctor seeks to reverse the effects and the cause of our illness, so too James gives us a prescription for reversing the influence and the dominance of sin in our lives.

Contrary to what is sometimes assumed, repentance is not a momentary act that takes place once for all at the beginning of the Christian life. True it has a beginning; but it is a life-long process. Luther was perhaps wiser than he knew when he posted his Ninety-Five Theses on the door of the Castle Church in Wittenberg on October 31, 1517 and made the first of them: 'When our Lord Jesus Christ said "repent" he meant that the whole of the Christian life should be repentance.'

John Calvin expressed the same truth, albeit in the different words of the title to the *Institutes* Book III, Chapter iii: 'Our Regeneration by faith: Repentance'. To the twenty-first century Bible student who is familiar with the Reformed theology that flows from Calvin, this title may seem odd. Faith is, surely, the fruit of regeneration, not the means by which it takes place. But for Calvin 'regeneration' (the divine renewal) continues throughout our whole life. Faith (trusting in Christ as Saviour and Lord), and repentance (turning away from sin to serve and obey him) have their starting point at the inauguration of this new life. But as Calvin rightly makes clear they continue until the day we see Christ face to face and are made wholly like him.

This explains why this section is book-ended in verses 6 and 10 by the verbs 'submit' and 'humble' . In our sin we have exalted self over God and acted as though we know better than he does. The first step towards our recovery involves a new disposition before the Creator of the universe who knows and wants what is best for us, and who is to be trusted implicitly and obeyed willingly and completely. This is true humility. But since we have lacked it—indeed shown the reverse of it—we now need to be brought low—to submit and humble ourselves before him.

This medicine is hard for us to take because it involves 'swallowing our pride'. But there is no hope of a cure without it.

What follows seems to continue James's echoes of the major temptation narratives of Adam and Eve in Eden (Gen. 3) and David in Jerusalem (2 Sam. 11). He calls us to do precisely what Adam, Eve, and David failed to do.

SUBMITTING TO GOD AND RESISTING THE DEVIL

In a few well-chosen words the serpent assaulted the reliability, the authority, and the graciousness of God's word (Gen. 3:1-5). He questioned the 'inspiration' of the message Adam had passed on to Eve ('Did God actually say …?'). He attacked its authority ('God said, "You shall not eat … lest you die". But the serpent said …"You will not surely die …"'). He also distorted its graciousness (God commanded 'You may surely eat of *every tree* of the garden, but of the tree of the knowledge of good and evil you shall not eat …' Gen. 2:16-17). He gave them all the trees to enjoy, and only one to refrain from eating. But the serpent hissed, 'Did God actually say, "You shall not eat of *any tree* in the garden"?'—the obvious implication being that there was surely a deep cynicism, a dark side in the character of a God who would set such a breathtaking display before their senses but then tell them that none of it was to be theirs.

Adam and Eve fell; for three basic reasons they failed to resist the devil. (i) They were deceived (1:16); (ii) they mistrusted the Father of lights, with whom there is no variation or shadow due to change, from whom comes every good and every perfect gift (1:17). And (iii) they rebelled against his good and gracious authority.

This explains our current situation. And since our sinful lifestyle has been characterized by disobedience to God and deception by the devil, the first steps on the way back must be those of bowing down before the Lord ('Submit yourselves therefore to God', 4:7), confessing our sin, and at the same time rejecting the lies about him the evil one has told us. James adds a remarkable and wonderful promise: 'Resist the devil, and he will flee from you'—just as he did from the Lord Jesus (Matt. 4:11)!

But alongside these exhortations we are given a welcome invitation: 'Draw near to God, and he will draw near to you' (4:8).

DRAW NEAR, CLEANSE, AND PURIFY

'Draw near' is language associated with coming into the temple to worship; clean hands and pure hearts are the prerequisite for doing so. The fact that the Mosaic sacrificial system, and the Levitical laws with all their liturgical regulations, were only pictures of the true and are now obsolete, does not mean that God himself has changed. He is eternally holy. The worship that Isaiah witnessed, and the adoring chant of praise to the thrice holy God he heard (Isa. 6:3), will be heard throughout all eternity (Rev. 4:8). Our God is unchangingly and eternally 'holy'. So, if only someone with 'clean hands and a pure heart' could 'ascend the hill of the LORD' in the days of the old covenant (Psa. 24:3-4), the same must be true in the days of the new covenant. Indeed, the clearer and fuller revelation of God in Christ simply intensifies that obligation (See Heb. 12:14; Rev. 21:27).

But what does this mean in practical terms?

BEING WRETCHED, MOURNING, AND WEEPING

James addresses his readers as 'sinners' and 'double-minded'. Since this is so, the medicine he prescribes comes with side-effects that can be unpleasant and even painful for us. For the transformation of sinners is not easily effected: 'Cleanse your hands, you sinners, and purify your hearts, you double-minded. Be wretched and mourn and weep. Let your laughter be turned to mourning and your joy to gloom' (4:8-9).

It is as though, with all the other remedial directives Dr James is prescribing for us, a spiritual emetic is included in the cure. The Spirit's purpose in convicting us of sin is always to lead us to Christ and the discovery that in him there is superabundant grace. While the effect of this is the joy of forgiveness, it also brings with it a deeper awareness of our own unworthiness. We realize afresh how wretched we are! Paul certainly did ('Wretched man that I am! Who will deliver me from this body of death?' Rom. 7:24).

At the beginning of the Christian life, our (false) laughter was turned into mourning and our (false) joy to gloom. But that continues to reverberate. So long as we remain sinners, mourning and weeping will recur. And this cycle will continue until the day dawns when 'all the ransomed church of God is saved to sin no more'.[1] But thank God, that day will come! So, it is not in despair, but in hope that James urges his friends: 'Humble yourselves before the Lord, and he will exalt you' (4:10). When we come in real repentance

---

[1] From the hymn by William Cowper (1731–1800), 'There is a fountain filled with blood'.

before the Lord, and let our laughter be turned into mourning we will discover with the psalmist

> You have turned for me my mourning into dancing;
>   you have loosed my sackcloth
>   and clothed me with gladness (Psa. 30:11).

We have already noticed in these studies that it is sometimes a challenge to understand why the mind of a New Testament author moves from one subject to another. Why does James now continue his letter by urging his readers 'Do not speak evil against one another, brothers' (4:11)?

To say, 'Because he was inspired by the Spirit' is true, but hardly helpful. It simply presses the question back a stage rather than answer it. It leaves us asking 'What is the connection in the mind of the Spirit between the themes of 4:1-10 and the theme of 4:11-12?'

The answer possibly lies in James's understanding of what is involved in repentance: it reverses a behaviour pattern that was entrenched in our lives and had become habitual to us and, sadly, characteristic of us. Repentance begins to produce good fruit where there was formerly only bad fruit.

Earlier James had written about being 'slow to anger' (1:19), about the abuse of the tongue (3:6), and in the opening words of this chapter about 'quarrels' (4:1). God 'gives more grace' and 'gives grace to the humble' (4:6) precisely to stem the flow of this tide of sin. Indeed, more than stem the flow, he reverses it.

The implication? James spells it out: 'Do not speak evil against one another, brothers' (4:11).

Notice how he uses the word *brother* three times in one verse here. Quite instinctively, unselfconsciously, James embraces his correspondents as his brothers and therefore as brothers to each other. The new birth of which he has already spoken (1:18) makes us firstfruits of his creation but also brings us into the Father's 'birth family'. Here is all the motivation we need to bless each other (i.e. to speak well of each other). We have the same Father because we have the same Saviour and the same Spirit. We have been brought to see our sinfulness and have mourned over it, and God has shown us more grace (4:6). To speak ill of each other would be utterly contrary to nature, that is the renewed nature we share in Christ.

But if this is true, James adds a further motivating argument: 'The one who speaks against a brother or judges his brother, speaks evil against the law and judges the law. But if you judge the law, you are not a doer of the law but a judge. There is only one lawgiver and judge, he who is able to save and to destroy. But who are you to judge your neighbour?' (4:11-12).

The reasoning here may seem intricate but with a little patience we can follow James's line of thought:

- The person who speaks against a brother speaks evil of the law because rather than being a doer of the law (and therefore a person who loves his neighbour) he is acting as though he were the judge rather than the judged.
- Such a person is, in essence, usurping a role that belongs to God himself. He alone is the lawgiver and judge.
- Who, then, do we think we are, judging a neighbour and thus arrogating to ourselves what is the sole prerogative of God?

But now that we have separated out these strands in James's logic we need to pause and reflect on them and examine ourselves in the light of them. For here James brings us back to a question God might well have asked Adam and Eve when they hid from his presence among the trees in the Garden of Eden, or asked David as he allowed his gaze to linger on Bathsheba. It is essentially the question Nathan the prophet posed to David with such alarming and awakening effect on him: *Who are you…?* Who do you think you are? You are the *judged*, not the *judge*! (See 2 Sam. 12:1-15.)

What is our answer to that question? It is that we are sinners who have lost sight of the fact that God is jealous to possess all there is to have of us. We have forgotten that God opposes the proud, and that it is to the humble that he gives grace. We need to take to heart these exhortations: 'Cleanse your hands … purify your hearts … Be wretched and mourn and weep … Humble yourselves … Do not speak evil' against your brothers.

Do you know who you are? Then you will thank God that in Jesus Christ 'he gives more grace'—because when we know who we are we realize that more grace is our greatest need.

I I

The Unpredictability of Life

Come now, you who say, 'Today or tomorrow we will go into such and such a town and spend a year there and trade and make a profit'— [14] *yet you do not know what tomorrow will bring. What is your life? For you are a mist that appears for a little time and then vanishes.* [15] *Instead you ought to say, 'If the Lord wills, we will live and do this or that.'* [16] *As it is, you boast in your arrogance. All such boasting is evil.* [17] *So whoever knows the right thing to do and fails to do it, for him it is sin.*

(James 4:13-17)

James has now reached a new stage in his letter, indicated by the way he seems to address specific groups of people in his scattered 'congregation' ('Come now, you who ... Come now, you ...' 4:13 and 5:1).

Some, perhaps many, of the original recipients of the letter were merchants. They were traders who earned their living—and in the past, perhaps, even their fortune—by buying and selling a variety of commodities. They developed their personal business strategies and, doubtless, it became instinctive to say: 'Today or tomorrow we will go into such and such a town and spend a year there and trade and make a profit.' Business-minded people can often calculate how long it will take to develop a marketplace. Forward planning is essential.

Developing a business plan may sound a very modern thing to do, but it as old as the Bible. And indeed, it is a commendable thing to do. The 'excellent wife' of Proverbs 31:10-31 is a woman who has a good business head on her shoulders and develops her strategy: she sees a field, thinks about what she could do with it, buys it, and then follows through on her plan to plant a profitable vineyard

(Prov. 31:16). Jesus seems to have assumed that it is simply a matter of wisdom for anyone thinking of a commercial venture to have a business plan to make it a success (Luke 14:28-29).

But while this is true it is important to remember that 'man proposes, God disposes' and to learn that we live in daily dependence upon the Lord and within the context of his providential watch-care over us.

We have a tendency to run ahead of God. It is all too possible to slip into a kind of practical atheism in the way we plan our lives. So, James reminds his first readers of a series of basic principles to which they need to return. All of us are frequently in danger of forgetting or neglecting them. These verses provide us with a valuable revision course.

Here, then, are four important principles.

THE UNCERTAINTY OF LIFE

In verse 13 we can almost see several merchants round a table, poring over a map of the Mediterranean area, excitedly planning where to go next in search of profit. The journey will take them so many days; establishing themselves and making the right contacts will take longer; but then once they have a foothold in the city they will prosper. Nothing has been left out of their detailed planning.

Why does James see a problem here? This is surely normal—and wise—business practice. But something is missing. Perhaps James knew the story his half-brother had told about a rich farmer (Luke 12:13-21)? He had a major business plan for the redevelopment of his plant with a view to exponential growth. But there was a problem. He did not reckon on God's timing. Whatever his profession of faith might have been he was living as a practical atheist. God was simply not in his thoughts (Psa. 10:4 KJV).

The problem is not that it is a mistake to make plans, far less that good business planning is sinful. It is failing to live before the face of God; failing to consider time in the light of eternity; failing to live conscious of the fact that our lives are in God's hands and not our own—this is the great mistake. These were men with an inadequate perspective on their lives: 'Today or tomorrow we will go ... spend a year ... trade and make a profit' (4:13). It is the underlying assumption that is so short-sighted; and of course, the problem with being short-sighted is that one cannot see into the distance. There is wisdom in making plans; but there is a false self-assurance in the easy assumption that we can go, spend, trade, and profit. It assumes we are in control; it is blind to the unpredictability of life; it takes no account of God's will. That is always a spiritual danger sign; it is never an expression of faith.

THE BREVITY OF LIFE

In verse 14, James calls for some self-reflection: 'What is your life?' He uses a common experience to give force to his point. A mist hangs over the land in the early morning; but then it soon disappears in the warm rays of the sun.

Life is like that. It is short. The older you get the more obvious it becomes that the years which once seemed to stretch out before you as though they would last indefinitely have passed so quickly and cannot be recaptured. The passage of time seems to accelerate; the breath of life begins to fade. These merchants were looking at their plans through the wrong end of the telescope. Life seemed long, eternity distant. The truth is the reverse: life is short, eternity is near. These merchants were setting their lives by a clock that was adjusted to a false view of time. If they were in fact Christians, they had forgotten Jesus' question: what profit is there in gaining the whole world if it means losing your soul in the pursuit of ephemeral gain (Matt 16:26)? They had lost sight of the necessity of thinking in terms of eternity-long sustainable growth and profit!

What was missing? James now puts his finger on the central problem:

EXCLUDING GOD'S WILL FROM LIFE

What lies at the heart of the problem James detected is thinking 'Here is what *we* have decided to do' without taking into consideration what *God* might be planning to do. The questions, 'What does God want?' and 'What will tend most to God's glory?', must always take absolute priority over the question, 'How can we make a profit?' It is right to plan ahead. That is biblical wisdom. But in Scripture it is always set within the context of recognizing God's sovereignty, being willing to yield to him, and seeking a plan of action that is consistent with his revealed will and aims to express his glory. In sharp contrast however, these merchants gave little or no recognition to the sovereign watch-care and overruling of God in their lives.

Rather, writes James, 'you ought to say, "If the Lord wills, we will live and do this or that"' (4:15). Nor is this merely a matter of adding 'D.V.' (*Deo volente*, i.e. 'God willing') to what we say or write. That can become a mere habit that borders on a neurosis, rather than an expression of obedient faith. No, this is a heart recognition that 'Many are the plans in the mind of a man, but it is the purpose of the Lord that will stand' (Prov. 19:21). Significantly the book of Proverbs links this to 'the fear of the LORD' (Prov. 19:23), implying that this is the characteristic attitude of the person who has gained wisdom.

We should notice here that the New Testament does not view this approach to life as belonging to any advanced standing in the Christian life. It is basic and fundamental. It is inscribed in the cardinal principles that come to expression in the Lord's Prayer: 'Your kingdom come, your will be done, on earth as it is in heaven' (Matt. 6:10). Jesus had already made plain what this means in practical terms. When Satan proposed a 'plan of action' to him in the wilderness, his response was to ask: 'What is the will of God in this matter?' His answer came straight out of the book of Deuteronomy: 'Man shall not live by bread alone, but by every word that comes from the mouth of God' (Matt. 4:4, citing Deut. 8:3). The folly of the merchants James addresses is that they were planning as though they did live on bread alone; they were making the same old mistake of interpreting their lives in the light of what they could see rather than in the light of what they had heard from God's word and wisdom. Temporal, not eternal, profit filled their minds.

But isn't this such a common attitude that, surely, we cannot regard it as being quite so serious? We have seen that James has a way of tearing off the masks that we wear and showing us ourselves in a more searching light. Once again, he does that here.

THE SELF-SUFFICIENCY THAT POISONS

The disposition James describes here was (and is) by no means limited to the merchant classes. It is commonplace—and therein lies the danger that we might think it must therefore be relatively harmless. Sadly, this is how we often judge things. As more people share an attitude or engage in an activity the old 'sinful' becomes the new 'normal'.

What is disconcerting is that we may notice this in some areas of life (sexual mores and gender distinctions come immediately to mind) but be blind to it in other areas. James's warnings alert us to the fact that we can be sensitive to the question 'What is God's will?' in one area but ignore it in other areas. For what concerns him in this context is that making our own plans without reference to God's will, far from being a relatively harmless failing, is in fact a poison that seriously damages our spiritual health.

Here the symptom to which James refers is 'you boast in your arrogance. All such boasting is evil' (4:16). This symptom may present itself in many different forms, some blatant and obvious, others less so. But the person who assumes that what he has accomplished has been achieved without reference to God will, to one degree or another, speak and act as a self-reliant person. And the more able they are the greater justification they will find for the way they approach life. In its crassest form they will openly boast: 'I did it my way'; in its subtler form they may say 'I am very thankful that I have been able to do this ....' But if someone were to ask, 'To whom are you thankful?' the answer would resolve into at best, 'those who have helped me to accomplish my goals, and especially myself'.

This is a diameter removed from the attitude to which the apostle Paul gave such eloquent expression. He was never a merchant (the tent-making industry was something he must have trained for in his youth but at no point in his life was it any more than an ancillary trade). But in other ways he had exuded the spirit of the self-made man as he indicates to the Galatians ('I was advancing ... beyond many of my own age ... so extremely zealous was I ...', Gal. 1:14) and to the Philippians, 'If anyone else thinks he has reason for confidence in the flesh, I have more ...' (Phil. 3:4). In Christ, however, all this changed. Now he could say: 'Far be it from me to boast except in the cross of our Lord Jesus Christ, by which the world has been crucified to me, and I to the world' (Gal. 6:14). This was what was lacking in these merchants. They needed to learn to live before the face of God. While their approach to their calling as businessmen might seem admirable or even enviable in the eyes of men, James tells us that in the sight of God it was 'arrogance' (4:16).

The principles at the heart of James's teaching here have an application to all Christians. But we should not gloss over the fact that it has a focus on people engaged in business. That is not an easy world—especially for a Christian. But for that very reason it is a sphere in which James's teaching underlines in very practical ways the difference Christ's transforming power makes not only to personal life but also to business life.

This brings James to his concluding application: 'So whoever knows the right thing to do and fails to do it, for him it is sin' (4:17).

Some commentators have been puzzled by the vigour of James's words and his judgement that the attitude of these businessmen is tantamount to arrogance. Is it possible that there could be genuine Christians who have such a this-worldly disposition? But when we bear in mind his exposure of other sins that ought not to be so (3:10), we will understand that the sins of these merchants are only one more form of the spiritual arrogance that lurks deep within the heart.

This is probably why James concludes this section by stating a general principle: 'whoever knows the right thing to do and fails to do it, for him it is sin'. If you know what the implications of the gospel are, but do not take them to heart, then you are sinning against God. You have already forgotten the warning James gave several chapters ago: 'Do not be deceived ... Every good gift and every perfect gift is from above' (1:16-17). We need to remember Paul's words: 'What do you have that you did not receive? If then you received it, why do you boast as if you did not receive it?' (1 Cor. 4:7).

12

The Danger of False Riches

Come now, you rich, weep and howl for the miseries that are coming upon you. [2] *Your riches have rotted and your garments are moth-eaten.* [3] *Your gold and silver have corroded, and their corrosion will be evidence against you and will eat your flesh like fire. You have laid up treasure in the last days.* [4] *Behold, the wages of the labourers who mowed your fields, which you kept back by fraud, are crying out against you, and the cries of the harvesters have reached the ears of the Lord of hosts.* [5] *You have lived on the earth in luxury and in self-indulgence. You have fattened your hearts in a day of slaughter.* [6] *You have condemned and have murdered the righteous person. He does not resist you.*

(James 5:1-6)

James has been like a physician examining a patient, patiently listing and analyzing our symptoms. 'Is it sore here?', he asks, 'What about here?' And just as a medical doctor may press on exactly the sore point, so James asks, 'Sore here?'—and we realize he sees the cause of the problem. In chapter 4 he put his finger on such sins as bitterness (4:1-3), spiritual adultery (4:4-6); double-mindedness and slander (4:7-12) and arrogance (4:13-17). And now, as he continues in 5:1-6, he puts his finger on another problem: *worldliness.*

The charge is serious, and we cannot fail to sense the righteous anger with which James pens these words. But who is he addressing in this strong language? Can these people possibly be professing Christians? He accuses them of such blatant sins that probably most modern commentators assume he is addressing people outside of the church. That may be the case, and if so it would be in keeping with the prophetic tradition. When, for example, Amos issues his series of 'law suits' against Israel's neighbours (Amos 1:3–2:3) he is not addressing them directly but speaking about them to his own people. It is possible that the citizens of Damascus, Gaza, Tyre, Edom, Ammon, and Moab (whom he addresses 'for three transgressions … and for four') never read or heard his words of condemnation and judgement.

Perhaps James fits into this same pattern. But perhaps not. It is all too easy to idealize the New Testament church. The mantra 'We need to get back to being like the New Testament church' needs to be qualified. Which New Testament church? Corinth with its excesses both moral and spiritual? Galatia with all its Judaizing problems?

An entire encyclopaedia of sins can be found in our hearts even after we have become Christians. Indeed, we are likely to be much more conscious of them than ever before, for the Spirit of God exposes sinful tendencies we never believed were present in us! It follows, therefore, that within the body of Christ to which we belong, there may be serious dysfunctions. Professing Christians may not always be practising Christians; we are never wholly consistent. A man who seems to be a saint in the fellowship may be engaging in serious sin outside of it. One only needs to think of the New Testament correspondence to find illustrations—not least Jesus' correspondence with the churches in the opening chapters of Revelation (Rev. 2:1–3:22). Alas, sin continues to be present in the contemporary church as well.

So perhaps we should not simply assume that James is addressing only those who are outside of the church. He speaks, as it were, as a witness for the prosecution. More than that, he seems to act also as the prosecuting counsel, the jury, and even as the judge. In a court case the charge is read, the prosecutor makes his case based on the evidence, the jury reaches its verdict, and the sentence is pronounced by the judge. Here, however, James's first words assume the verdict. He then cites the evidence for it, and finally indicates the consequences.

THE CHARGE AND THE JUDGEMENT

James portrays the consequences of the verdict and the sentence of condemnation that follows as though it were taking place before the eyes of the accused—perhaps it was. The very treasures that the rich had reserved for themselves lose their value. Everything the greedy and self-serving rich have amassed as an expression of their self-worth eventually disintegrates.

These words are intended to open our eyes to the true value of things. We have seen before that part of James's pastoral burden is to point out how easily our senses deceive us. We mistakenly assume we see things exactly the way they are. But he wants us to 'see' and even to feel things as they really are. There is a dramatic intensity in his words. We can apply them to modern life:

> Look now at what you thought of as riches—they are infected with rot. Look at those overvalued garments—the designer jeans, the expensive suit, the dress hanging in the closet—they spoke volumes about your self-image and your wealth. But now look at them—they are disintegrating before your eyes. The moths have eaten them.
>
> Go on then, down to your private bank. Open the vault where you store your gold and silver. They have all corroded (5:3)! Worse, that corrosion affects not only what you have but what you are. It will eat your flesh like fire.

In their own eyes, and perhaps also in others' estimation, the resources they had amassed seemed strong and substantial. But they had failed to see their corrosive effect. They had set their hearts on ephemeral things when their souls could be satisfied only by eternal things. Their riches were perishing before their eyes.

'You have laid up treasure in the last days' (5:3b), says James. He sees this fact not as an ameliorating element in their sin but an exacerbation of it. What does he mean? What is the connection between verses 2-3a and 3b?

These words press home the seriousness of their sin. Despite the fact that they are living in the last days they have ignored the implications.

The expression 'the last days' refers not to some future period but to the new age inaugurated by Christ's death, resurrection, ascension, and the sending of the Holy Spirit. Peter made this clear in his sermon on the Day of Pentecost. The coming of the Spirit marked the beginning of the last days, just as Joel had prophesied (Joel 2:28; Acts 2:17; cf. Heb. 1:2).

James is therefore underlining how serious and heinous their sin is. For it is despite the full revelation of God in Jesus Christ who brought life and immortality to light through the gospel (2 Tim. 1:10) that these people have hoarded up earthly treasures! His presupposition is since they were living in the last days they should have developed a certain detachment from this world's goods and held their possessions with a light touch and an open hand (cf. 1 Cor.7:29-31).

We may respond to a passage like this by moving on to the next section. After all, we are not among the rich. Yet James's warning applies more generally. For it arises out of Jesus' admonition that we should all lay up treasure in heaven rather than on earth (Matt. 6:19-21). And he added that what tells you where your treasure lies is what you set your heart on, what you tend to think about when there is nothing else about which you need to think.

Imagine this scenario in a church today: the preacher has just finished his third sermon in a series on 'Living in the Last Days'. The congregation stands to sing:

> Jesus, thou joy of loving hearts,
>   Thou fount of life, thou light of men
> From the best bliss that earth imparts,
>   We turn unfilled to thee again.[1]

Or, perhaps, in a less traditional setting:

> All I once held dear, built my life upon
> All this world reveres, and wars to own
> All I once thought gain I have counted loss,
> Spent and worthless now, compared to this:
> Knowing you, Jesus;
> Knowing you, there is no greater thing …[2]

But then the person beside you sits down, and opens up the bank app on his smart phone—and while the phone is in his hands, he checks the day's special deals on Amazon. Hardly a serious

---

[1] Attributed to Bernard of Clairvaux (1091–1153), tr. R. Palmer.
[2] Graham Kendrick (1950–).

crime! After all, he is not one of the rich. And yet it speaks volumes about his attachment to this world, and his detachment from the last days. Are we similarly impacted?

Just as James has taught us positively to live the present in the light of the future, so here he uses the same principle to warn us of spiritual danger. Nor does he do this in a take-it-or-leave-it fashion. He wants his readers to feel the truth of what he is writing, and to touch their affections in order to draw them back from their sin. 'Look at this!' he seems to be saying, and 'Come now, you rich, weep and howl for the miseries that are coming upon you' (5:1).

If it is true that he is echoing the spirit of the Old Testament prophets here, it is even more true that he is echoing the words of the Lord Jesus in Matthew 6:19-24. He is also underlining the vital principle we have seen enshrined in the New Testament's approach to Christian living. Believers are called to live their lives backwards from the judgement seat of Christ, in the light of God's assessment, not in the light of this world's perspective on what makes a man or woman rich. Tragically these people were in danger of laying up treasures on earth rather than in heaven. But John Newton was right:

> Fading is the worldling's pleasure,
> All his boasted pomp and show;
> Solid joys and lasting treasure
> None but Zion's children know.[1]

FURTHER EVIDENCE AND ADMONITION

James brings further specific charges against these rich people. It is one thing to hoard wealth. But, in addition, they oppress the poor. They have failed to pay workmen the wages they are due—'the wages of the labourers who mowed your fields ... you kept back by fraud' (5:4). This, in a subsistence society for men who were farm labourers doing piecework with no contract, placed the health and well-being of whole families in jeopardy. Meanwhile these wealthy employers have lived 'in luxury and in self-indulgence' (5:5).

God cares about the poor (Deut. 24:15); these men care only about profit margins and are guilty of fraud (5:4). If these rich people are professing Christians, they are yet to grasp what the grace of God really is. His desire is to bless those who serve him.

[1] From the hymn 'Glorious Things of Thee Are Spoken'.

In the nature of the case, the business owner must bear in mind the 'profit motive'. But that should be subservient to the 'blessing motive' directed towards those whom he employs. They, after all, bless him. And the result of such a counter-cultural orientation is likely to be that they will want even more to be a blessing to the company.

The reverse was true in this case. And the result was that rather than lifting their voices to God in thankfulness for their employer, 'the cries of the harvesters have reached the ears of the Lord of hosts' (5:4).

Two aspects of this statement are worth noting.

The first is the way it echoes passages in the Old Testament. Remember God's response to Cain's question 'Am I my brother's keeper?': 'The voice of your brother's blood is crying to me from the ground' (Gen. 4:10). Nothing is hidden from him. He sees all the evidence and his judgement will be according to the truth (Rom. 2:1-11).

But James's words also seem to echo Exodus 2:23-25. The Israelites in bondage in Egypt were crying to the Lord to rescue them from slavery. They did not know that 'God knew'. He not only 'heard their groaning' but was already preparing Moses to deliver them and was planning to send judgement on their oppressors.

James implies that God is still doing the same. Not only so, but (a second aspect of these words) he is doing so as 'the Lord of hosts' (5:4). He is the King of the armies of heaven. He will come in judgement on his enemies.

But James has not yet finished his terrible indictment. There is more. The rich 'have lived on the earth in luxury and in self-indulgence'. But what does he mean by saying, 'You have fattened your hearts in a day of slaughter' (5:5)? What exactly is this 'day of slaughter'?

In the light of what he says in the following verse this could refer to the fact that they 'have condemned and murdered the righteous person' (5:6—a statement which is also open to more than one interpretation). But perhaps he is further emphasizing the gulf between their perception of things and the reality of the situation. They see themselves as grain farmers making a profit. But the truth presents a different picture. Their defrauding of their harvest employees spells profit for them. But in fact, they are feeding on their sin, not realizing that they are fattening themselves up for the day of slaughter, the day of God's judgement.

There is still more: 'You have condemned and murdered the righteous person. He does not resist you' (5:6). 'But surely,' the rich man might say, 'it is one thing to accuse me of fraud, quite another to accuse me of murder. Perhaps I should plead partly guilty to the first charge—although you must remember that I do need to make a profit! But I am certainly not guilty of murder!'

James, however, has already traced the way in which actions lead to consequences (1:14-15). And we never break only one commandment at a time. Fraud leads to hunger; hunger to starvation; starvation to death. To defraud is to steal. To steal is to deprive someone of what belongs to their life; to do so is murder by intent. And if it leads to starvation it is murder in reality.

James's words refer to a rural economy and to a subsistence society. But they are relevant to the now dominant urban economies. We might think they could only apply to a privately owned business. It is doubtful if James would have seen things that way. At the end of the day every business is owned and run by people: share-holders and board members, CEOs, CFOs, COOs, by presidents and vice-presidents, by team leaders, managers, and others. It is now a more complex world in which to apply the principle that the labourer deserves his hire. But it is still the divine rule, and insofar as we have either a voice or a responsibility for others we need to find ways of blessing rather than cursing those who work for us. A minimum wage can be mandated by government legislation, but not the desire to bless. That comes through evangelical obedience to the legislation of the God who has blessed us in Christ (Eph.1:3). And therefore, not to want to bless the harvesters was a denial of both the law and the gospel.

Perhaps another alarm bell is sounded by the words of verse 6: 'you have condemned and murdered the righteous person. He does not resist you.' They have their most frequent fulfilment today, alas, in abortion procedures that carry the backing of local and national legislatures, and it seems public opinion. Since the landmark Roe *v* Wade decision of the Supreme Court of the United States, abortion procedures equivalent in number to twice the population of Australia have taken place. It has become a 'human right'. But this is exactly what the rich farmers of James's day thought too. They believed themselves to be 'clear thinking and clear seeing' about their rights.

Applications and admonitions usually follow expositions. Here the order is reversed perhaps because James sees the need to awaken some of his readers from their deep spiritual slumber. Like a military bugler playing *Reveille*, he issues a loud summons to acknowledge, confess, and repent of our sins: 'Come now, you rich, weep and howl for the miseries that are coming upon you.' This is the only response that is appropriate. See sin for what it is; see yourself for what you really are; catch sight of the judgement you deserve; be broken down in shame and sorrow. It is still true that—

> With sorrow for sin
> Doth repentance begin.

So here is what we need to reflect on:

- Re-examine your wealth—are you hoarding it or using it?

- Re-examine your debts to anyone who does any work for you—do you pay your bills quickly?

- Re-examine your attitude—do you want to bless those who work for you?

- Re-examine your vision—are you seeing things as they really are?

- And remember the words of Jesus in Revelation 3:17-20:

> 'You say, I am rich, I have prospered, and I need nothing, not realizing that you are wretched, pitiable, poor, blind, and naked. I counsel you to buy from me gold refined by fire, so that you may be rich, and white garments so that you may clothe yourself and the shame of your nakedness may not be seen, and salve to anoint your eyes, so that you may see. Those whom I love, I reprove and discipline, so be zealous and repent. Behold, I stand at the door and knock. If anyone hears my voice and opens the door, I will come in to him and eat with him, and he with me.'

13

Patience Until Christ Returns

Be patient, therefore, brothers, until the coming of the Lord. See how the farmer waits for the precious fruit of the earth, being patient about it, until it receives the early and the late rains. [8] You also, be patient. Establish your hearts, for the coming of the Lord is at hand. [9] Do not grumble against one another, brothers, so that you may not be judged; behold, the Judge is standing at the door. [10] As an example of suffering and patience, brothers, take the prophets who spoke in the name of the Lord. [11] Behold, we consider those blessed who remained steadfast. You have heard of the steadfastness of Job, and you have seen the purpose of the Lord, how the Lord is compassionate and merciful. [12] But above all, my brothers, do not swear, either by heaven or by earth or by any other oath, but let your 'yes' be yes and your 'no' be no, so that you may not fall under condemnation.

(James 5:7-12)

Here is an interesting Bible quiz question: Which New Testament author was the first to know Jesus? Perhaps our instincts would be to think of Peter rather than Paul, John rather than Matthew. The answer? Our author James, the half-brother of Jesus. They lived together for several decades. It therefore should not surprise us if nature (if he was Mary's son), nurture, and then grace all resulted in James showing some decided similarities to Jesus. Certainly, we find many echoes of Jesus' teaching in this letter. And are there also some indications of family resemblances? After all, they both would have grown up to manhood under the same human influences. It would make a worthwhile group or family Bible study to read through this whole letter to try to spot all the similarities.

James has been leading us along the pathway to Christian maturity. We grow through being tested, through the impact of God's word on us, and through living consistent Christian lives. James has written as a spiritual physician, surgeon, and lawyer. Now he urges us to learn to live according to God's timetable, not man's—and certainly not our own.

If we are to do so we need to be patient and steadfast. This terminology appears several times within a few verses. Four times, in verses 7, 8, and 10, James refers to being 'patient'; twice in verse 11 he refers to the importance of 'steadfastness'. These are qualities that need to be developed in us—not least if we are to live faithfully through times of stress. But they do not appear overnight; we cannot simply turn them on at will. They need to be developed over a lifetime. How does this happen? How does a Christian develop this quality of 'stickability'?

THE NATURE OF THE CHRISTIAN LIFE

Until Christ comes we need to be patient. James uses an illustration drawn from the familiar lifestyle of agrarian Palestinian life where the rains in October were followed by later rainfalls in November ('the early and the late rains'). The farmer sows his seed; but then he must wait for the ground to be watered. He needs to be patient.

James varies his vocabulary for patience. As he had done earlier in the letter (in 1:2-3, 12) he uses the word *hupomonē* which conveys the idea of being able to remain underneath a burden—like an Olympic weightlifter holding above his head a barbell so heavy that it would crush ordinary untrained men. The same expression is used in 5:11.

But in 5:7, 'be patient' translates a different, but no less picturesque Greek word: *makrothumeō*, literally, 'be long-tempered'. It is used more frequently in Scripture of God's attitude than it is of man's. It conveys the idea of someone who is not easily irritated or diverted.

Like his half-brother, James points to events in the natural world to illustrate life in the kingdom of God. What enables the farmer to wait? He knows that anxiety will not bring the early rain any earlier, nor will frustration accelerate the arrival of the late rains. Being irritated will not cause a cloud to come over the horizon. He knows that God continues to govern nature in a way that is usually regular. He also knows, however, that he is dependent on God for the rains. In a sense, once he has done his duty, there is nothing left for him to do. His responsibility now is simply to wait upon God. So, patience is the fruit of trust in God. The farmer learns patience as he lives his life in accordance with God's promises on the one hand (he will give both sun and rain) and God's providence and its rhythms on the other. He learns to wait 'for the precious fruit of the earth' (5:7).

So it must be with the Christian who wants to live a stable and mature Christian life.

If there is a secret to Christian patience it is a deep conviction about God's character, especially in three respects: (i) the absolute sovereignty of God's reign over all things—he 'works all things according to the counsel of his will' (Eph. 1:11); (ii) the perfect wisdom of God's providence through all things—he is 'the only wise God' (Rom. 16:27); (iii) the fatherly love of God for his children in all things—if he 'did not spare his own Son but gave him up for us all', we can be sure he will 'graciously give us all things' along with him (Rom. 8:32).

If we know that this is true, then we are able to entrust our circumstances and cares into his hands, to believe that both his ways and his timing are perfect, and that we can therefore wait for his plan to unfold safe in the loving grip of our heavenly Father. Anxiety breeds impatience; faith breeds a resting spirit that is prepared to wait on the Lord while it waits *for* the Lord.

On this basis, James issues two imperatives.

(i) 'Establish your hearts' (5:8). Stability may not be a spectacular grace, but it is a vital one. It was one of Jesus' concerns for his disciples (John 14:1), just as it was one of the goals of apostolic ministry to promote it (see Eph. 4:9-14). Infants are unsteady on their feet. Stability and balance are marks of maturity.

But there is surely something enigmatic about the reason he gives for this command: 'for the coming of the Lord is at hand' (5:8b).

What is the force of what James says here? Is he concerned that the expectation of the return of Christ might create a destabilizing excitement—just as it did in some members of the Thessalonian church (2 Thess. 2:1ff.)? More likely, he sees the coming (*parousia*) of the Lord as both an encouragement and a motive for stability. It is 'at hand' in the sense that it is the next great event on the divine calendar. Until then God will continue to work out his purposes and bring them to completion on the day of Jesus Christ (Phil. 1:6). In addition, only then will it become clear exactly what pattern God has been weaving into our lives and more broadly into the story of the church. Knowing that this is the case we learn to 'wait eagerly' even if we also 'groan inwardly' for that day to come (cf. Rom. 8:23).

Children on a road trip often find that the last few miles of the journey seem to be the slowest and longest of all. They need ongoing reassurance—'we're almost there'—in order to remain patient. So it is in the Christian journey. We are 'almost there'. In the days when our patience is tested and there are pressures and burdens that threaten our stability, this is the word to remember! And what a day it will be when God completes the tapestry he has been weaving throughout history. Surely it will have been worth waiting for!

But then James adds a second exhortation that seems to come from nowhere! First 'Establish your hearts', then 'Do not grumble' (5:9). Is there any connection between these two statements?

(ii) 'Do not grumble against one another' may seem totally disconnected from the previous imperative. But think of your own childhood road trips. Were you ever in the back seat with your brother or sister? When the journey seemed long, nothing much seemed to be happening, and you became listless—what happened? Were there sibling squabbles in the back seat? So it is sometimes in the church family—things seem to be going nowhere, or have even taken a wrong turning—and we feel the stress; we are no longer patient, resting in God's loving sovereignty and wisdom. It is just then that we are likely to grumble against one another.

This was what happened in the wilderness wanderings, as the sad narrative of Numbers chapter 11 records. It was a danger Paul saw lurking at the door of the church family in Philippi (Phil. 2:14). Perhaps this explains why James speaks not only about 'the coming of the Lord' (5:7, 8) but also says it 'is at hand' (5:8). The return of Christ may still lie in the distant future; but he is not far away. Even now he is standing at the door as the Judge who will right all wrongs (5:9). Indeed he stands at the door and knocks (Rev. 3:20). He is in the car with us on the journey, as it were. Knowing this is the great solvent. As we learn the practice of the presence of Christ, and wait for him, serving each other begins to take the place of grumbling.

Notice again how James refers to his half-brother: he is 'Lord' (5:7, 8) and 'Judge' (5:9). Here again, in a matter-of-fact way, he makes crystal clear his convictions about Jesus' identity.

EXAMPLES

We learn by example. Theological reasoning helps us to understand how the gospel works. A personal example, however, helps us to see what it looks and sounds like, and enables us to apply its lessons to our own lives. This is surely one of the reasons the Bible is full not only of narrative but of biographies too. We sometimes find it difficult to read God's handwriting in our lives. But in biblical biographies he writes the principles of his grace in large letters to help us to read them. Perhaps James learned this 'Do you see how these principles work out in real life situations?' from Jesus as well as from the Old Testament. But however he learned it, he well understood it. Here he provides two illustrations of the patience and steadfastness he is urging on his readers.

(i) The first example is found in the prophets in general. What characterized their lives was suffering and patience (*makrothumia*, 5:10). Paul spoke about suffering producing patience in the sense of *hupomonē*—being able to take the strain, our spiritual muscle strength being built up by exercise and pressure. But that stress also requires and increases *makrothumia* 'long-temper', the kind of patience that can cope with difficult, painful, unresolved and frustrating situations (and people!).

In fact, the biographies of the prophets clarify an important principle: developing patience requires us to experience situations that bring pressure to bear on us and create stress. A Christian who has an outburst of impatience (short-temper) may say, 'I don't understand that; I am usually a very patient person.' But the truth is he or she is, in fact, an impatient person who has never been seriously tested! Stressful situations or people are the only way such patience develops. The prophets illustrate this. That is why we think of them as 'blessed' (5:11).

(ii) James's second illustration is more specific. The 'patience of Job' (5:11, KJV) is proverbial. But at times Job seems less than 'patient'—after all, he 'cursed the day of his birth' (Job 3:1). Here our limited understanding of what patience is may mislead us. James is not thinking of a passive, quietist element in Job's personality but rather his 'stickability', his gutsy determination to endure—his *hupomonē*. At times it looked as though—weightlifter like—his knees would buckle. But no, the weight-bearing bar was lifted above his head and, although his whole body trembled, by God's grace he managed to take the strain. James is not writing about natural temperament but about the spiritual strength that is built into us by God's providential dealings with us.

Do these examples fill us with trepidation? In fact, they are meant to encourage us because we 'have seen the purpose of the Lord, how the Lord is compassionate and merciful' (5:11). The word 'purpose' here translates the Greek word *telos* (goal, end, or purpose) We are encouraged by these examples because we can read the story backwards from its conclusion. The Scriptures give us hindsight on the lives of others so that we may have foresight on our own.

The suffering prophets and the agonized Job found God's providence hard to read; his purpose seemed obscured. There was little in their circumstances that suggested God was compassionate and merciful. No doubt Satan sought to drive them to despair. But while they could not see the *telos*, the end and goal God had in mind, they held on to the lesson enshrined in the story of Joseph, that God works things together for our good and for his glory (Gen. 45:5-8; 50:20; Rom. 8:28). That is what builds long-temper!

By contrast with Job and the prophets, we now know the whole of their life-stories. We see the *telos*, the purpose of the Lord (5:11), and the patterns and paths by which God brought them to it. So, in the midst of stress remember, James says, God always has a *telos* in view.

This is another reason why it is so important to remember that 'the coming of the Lord is at hand'. For although at the moment we may not understand, he promises that afterwards we will (John 13:7).

But where does verse 12 fit in all this? 'But above all, my brothers, do not swear, either by heaven or by earth or by any other oath, but let your "yes" be yes and your "no" be no, so that you may not fall under condemnation.' At first sight this seems a random, disconnected statement that James has thrown in. Is it only a suddenly remembered saying of Jesus? The words are indeed virtually a repetition of Matthew 5:34–37.

Some commentators see these words as the beginning of James's conclusion and therefore as an introduction or at least a bridge to verses 13 to 20. This may well be the case. Yet there seems to be a logical connection to what has preceded (in 5:7-11), for James introduces verse 12 with the words 'But above all ...'

What possible connection is there between the exhortations 'Be patient' and 'Do not grumble' and now 'do not swear ... let your "yes" be yes and your "no" be no, so that you may not fall under condemnation'? And why is this 'above all'?

Perhaps this: patience and endurance develop only in a context of friction and pressure. If we are impatient it is likely we will begin to grumble (5:9). We may also be tempted to ease the pressure or escape the suffering by compromised speech, choosing personal safety rather than Christian integrity. Remember Peter. Untested, he was confident that he would never deny Jesus, not even on pain of death (Luke 22:33). But in the event, it took only the insistent questioning of a servant girl and some bystanders to expose him for what he really was—a man who could not take the strain (Matt. 26:69-75).

This is the double-mindedness against which James warned his first readers (1:8; 4:8). It is a word in season to us to remain steadfast under trial. If so we will need to heed James's exhortation to be patient. We, like Peter, need to hear this counsel: 'Establish your hearts, for the coming of the Lord is at hand' (5:8).

As we read these words we may be inclined to feel that James is being stern and unfeeling, when what we need is the gentle touch. If so, ponder a repeated detail in this paragraph. Three times (5:7, 10, 12) James addresses his readers as 'brothers'. He does not use the term as a kind of verbal punctuation mark as some older Christians used to do. In common with other New Testament writers he tends to address his readers as 'brothers' as he moves from one concern about them to another, and to express that deep affection for them which undergirds the concerns he expresses (1:2, 16, 19; 2:1, 14; 3:1, 10; 4:11; 5:7, 10, 12, 19). It is an indication of his love for those he is addressing, and expresses his desire for them to work out the salvation God is working in them (Phil. 2:12-13). For if they were his brothers they were also the brothers of his half-brother, destined by God to be conformed to his image 'in order that he might be the firstborn among many brothers' (Rom. 8:29). No wonder, then, that his appeals to them are so full of concern!

14

The Needs of God's People

Is anyone among you suffering? Let him pray. Is anyone cheer-
ful? Let him sing praise. ¹⁴ Is anyone among you sick? Let him
call for the elders of the church, and let them pray over him,
anointing him with oil in the name of the Lord. ¹⁵ And the
prayer of faith will save the one who is sick, and the Lord will
raise him up. And if he has committed sins, he will be forgiven.
¹⁶ Therefore, confess your sins to one another and pray for one
another, that you may be healed. The prayer of a righteous
person has great power as it is working. ¹⁷ Elijah was a man
with a nature like ours, and he prayed fervently that it might
not rain, and for three years and six months it did not rain on
the earth. ¹⁸ Then he prayed again, and heaven gave rain, and
the earth bore its fruit.
¹⁹ My brothers, if anyone among you wanders from the truth
and someone brings him back, ²⁰ let him know that whoever
brings back a sinner from his wandering will save his soul from
death and will cover a multitude of sins.

(James 5:13-20)

I n the days when people conducted frequent correspondence with
each other, their letters often had a regular pattern. They began
slowly and wrote expansively, and then either as they came to the
end of a sheet of paper, knew that the mail would soon be collect-
ed, or simply ran out of energy, letters would end with a series of
staccato-like statements either giving news about people or brief
comments on a variety of issues.

Several New Testament letters share this pattern. They deal with
important doctrinal or pastoral issues, and they regularly close with

either news of fellow Christians or simple exhortations or comments on various issues. The Letter of James follows that pattern.

For James the Christian life involves personal and practical transformation.

Faith in Christ makes a practical difference in our lives. And it grows strong through the nourishment it receives from trusting and obeying God's word, and by being tested and tried. Sometimes James's words have been white hot; but it is as a brother to brothers that he has spoken. Now he has some concluding counsel for his brethren. He writes as though he were envisaging them sitting listening to his letter being read as a sermon preached in their worship service (in many ways that is exactly what it is). In his imagination he scans the faces in the congregation and reflects on their varying situations and needs. He has a kind of 'preaching grid' in his mind and makes sure that he has some practical counsel for Christians in various conditions and situations. Wisely he is conscious that if all he issues are rebukes then the needy and sensitive may be left at the end only nursing their wounds. No doubt he knew well that sometimes it is those who least need to be broken down who feel the devastating power of the preached word most keenly. And so he addresses the situations of four different groups: the suffering, the happy, the sick, and the backslider.

SUFFERING

What does James have to say 'When Bad Things Happen to Good People'?[1] No doubt James was theologically shrewd enough to know that there has only ever been one truly good person to whom bad things happened. Yet he knows that his Hebrew Bible often wrestled with the question, what do we say when bad things happen to God's people? They also experience suffering. That fact is implicit in the very verse that has probably brought most comfort to Christians in their suffering: 'We know that for those who love God all things work together for good, for those who are called according to his purpose' (Rom. 8:28). But the implication is that there are 'bad things' and they do not necessarily work for good on their own. If Paul had the story of Joseph in view when he wrote these words (he

---

[1] The title of a best-selling book by Harold S. Kushner (New York: Schocken Books, 1981).

seems to be echoing Gen. 50:20), then clearly there were many 'bad things' that God made to 'work together' in his life.

What should we do? James's answer is a single word: 'pray'. But it surely raises another question in our minds: What should we pray? He does not seem to answer that question. But here again we should remind ourselves of our important principle: if Scripture provides everything necessary 'that the man of God may be complete, equipped for every good work' (2 Tim. 3:16–17), then we should begin with Scripture itself to find the answers. And usually we find them in the very context that prompted our question. In fact, James had already told us what to pray for in the opening sections of his message:

- We should pray that we will be able to count it all joy when we meet trials of various kinds (1:2).
- We should pray that we will receive wisdom in order to respond to our situation in a way that glorifies God (1:5).
- We should pray that we will have the kind of endurance we will need to be patient when facing trials (1:12).
- We should pray that we will recognize what is happening when we are tempted, and be given strength to resist, rather than be deceived (1:13-16).
- We should pray that the Lord will sustain and strengthen our conviction that he is an unchanging God of light, and he gives us good gifts (1:17).

Yes, we always experience weakness and 'do not know what to pray for as we ought'. We are reliant on the work of the Spirit (Rom. 8:26). But there are also times when the reason we do not know is because we have failed to search the Scriptures. We should not expect God to provide us with individual revelation to guide us when he has already given it to us all in his word!

CHEERFUL

'Is anyone cheerful?' (5:13; the verb is translated 'take heart' in Acts 27:22, 25 and as 'encouraged' in Acts 27:36. The Greek physician and medical author Hippocrates, 460–370 BC, after whom the Hippocratic Oath is named, used it of a patient being 'in good heart'.)

It is an interesting question for more than one reason. For one thing it is not the kind of question a melancholic preacher would be likely to ask a congregation! James was obviously a deeply serious man; but he was not a pessimist. He could not have asked the question with any personal integrity unless he himself was cheerful.

So, what are you to do when you are cheerful? You should sing praise to God. But why is this important? For at least two reasons:

(i) Because singing praise is a joyful recognition that the Lord is the source of all our blessings. It is from him that every good and perfect gift comes to us (1:17). And praising him is a recognition that you have learned the lesson that children are taught in Sunday School:

> Count your blessings,
>   Name them one by one!
> And it will surprise you
>   What the Lord has done.

(ii) But singing praise for our blessings also saves us from a kind of idolatry in which we take the gift but then forget the Giver, because it turns our affections towards the Lord.

But does it really matter if we sing or not? In an obvious sense, yes—because we are commanded to do it in God's word both here and in other places (e.g. Psa. 30:4; 147:7; Eph. 5:19; Col. 3:16). But in addition to that, singing is not only an expression of our thoughts but also of our affections. It is the outflow of our meditation and admiration. And it has the effect of permeating our personality and lending an attractiveness to our spirits.

Are you a singing, cheerful Christian? Do you see this is an imperative?

So, if you are suffering, *pray*; if you are in good heart, *sing*.

But what if you are sick?

SICK

'Is anyone among you sick?' asks James. 'Let him call for the elders of the church' (5:14).

This is a surprise! But is it not also bad advice? There were physicians in James's day, even if they had neither the knowledge nor the resources of medical doctors today. Why not call them?

We should not here mistakenly think that positive statements necessarily imply comprehensive negatives: 'call for the elders' does not necessarily imply 'do not consult a medical practitioner'! To assume so would be to commit a logical fallacy.

Presumably James assumed his fellow Christians would seek whatever normal medical help was available. Paul seems to have been glad, perhaps even relieved, whenever Dr Luke travelled with him on his missionary journeys. And he recommended that Timothy 'No longer drink only water, but use a little wine for the sake of [his] stomach and [his] frequent ailments' (1 Tim. 5:23).

But the New Testament also recognizes that it is not the doctor who heals us. He may examine us, accurately diagnose our condition, prescribe medicine for us, or even recommend surgery to us. Through such processes we may be restored to health. But in the last analysis the physician enables our healing; he or she does not actually heal us. It is the Lord who heals us through his providential governing of our lives (whether by wine for our stomachs, medicine in them, or surgery on them).

The instinct to consult the physician for help is entirely proper. But it is also vital to look to the Lord for healing. That is always true. And for a variety of unspecified reasons James urges those who are sick to call for the elders of the church (5:14) so that they may pray over them and anoint them with oil. This is not what Roman Catholics call 'Extreme Unction' (or today, the 'Anointing of the Sick') given in serious illness, usually for the final part of life's journey. James has recovery in mind, not death. What is it then?

It is, first of all, evidently a regular and repeated activity in the local church. James sees this prayer and anointing as part of the responsibility of the ordinary leaders and under-shepherds in the congregation. This is not one of those gifts that Paul describes as 'signs of a true apostle' (2 Cor. 12:12). It is not a special and individual gift of healing (1 Cor. 12:9, 28, 30), but a part of what James saw as the ongoing ministry of local church elders. It has a simple and unostentatious pattern.

The sick person first calls the elders. This is a basic acknowledgement of need. James hints that as the elders gather they do so in fellowship with the sick person. In this context he writes: 'Therefore confess your sins to one another and pray for one another, that you may be healed' (5:16). This is neither 'the sacrament of the anointing of the sick' or 'extreme unction' nor a justification for priestly confession. For the expressions 'to one another' and 'for one another' make clear that what takes place is a mutual recognition of our faults and sins, with a mutual desire to enjoy forgiveness and the fellowship this effects.

In this context, the elders pray over the sick person and anoint him with oil. Oil was used as a healing agent in antiquity. The good Samaritan knew that it would give relief to the cut and bruised man on the Jericho Road (Luke 10:34). But here the more natural meaning of the anointing is that it served as a sign of God's grace, consecrating the individual to the Lord and to the work of his Spirit.

It is also evident that healing is not automatic, nor indeed is it the anointing that heals. Rather, 'the prayer of faith will save the one who is sick, and the Lord will raise him up' (5:15).

This is the only place in Scripture where the expression the 'prayer of faith' is used, and the only reference to this ministry of the elders. What does James mean?

We should notice first that James seems to draw a parallel between:

'the prayer of faith will save the one who is sick' (5:15)

and

'the prayer of a righteous person has great power as it is working' (5:16)

He then illustrates this and gives us clues to understanding what he means by pointing to Elijah: 'Elijah was a man with a nature like ours, and he prayed fervently that it might not rain, and for three years and six months it did not rain on the earth. Then he prayed again, and heaven gave rain, and the earth bore its fruit' (5:17-18).

Here James takes us behind the scenes of 1 Kings 17:1–18:46. He understands that all of Elijah's actions were governed by God's word, including the terrible destruction of the prophets of Baal (in obedience to Deut. 13:1-5, 13-18; 17:2-7). The fact that rain came in response to Elijah's prayers (1 Kings 18:41-46) implies that the rain had also first ceased in response to his earlier prayers.

We are to envisage Elijah taking God's covenant promise of judgement back to him in prayer and asking him to fulfil it:

> Lord, you promised in your word: 'Take care lest your heart be deceived, and you turn aside and serve other gods and worship them; then the anger of the LORD will be kindled against you, and he will shut up the heavens, so that there will be no rain, and the land will yield no fruit ...' (Deut. 11:16-17; cf. 28:15, 23).
>
> Now, O Lord, keep your covenant, fulfil your promise and act! Shut up the heavens!

In the confidence that God would honour his word, Elijah had boldly appeared before Ahab and said, 'As the LORD, the God of Israel, lives, before whom I stand, there shall be neither dew nor rain these years, except by my word' (1 Kings 17:1). Elijah's word was simply God's word trusted in faith and God's promises claimed in prayer.

The 'prayer of faith' then is not something that we work up from within. Rather it is our bringing God's promises back to him, asking him to keep them, and trusting that he will. It involves the Spirit-wrought conviction that those promises apply to our needs.

But what of the words, 'And the prayer of faith will save the one who is sick, and the Lord will raise him up. And if he has committed sins, he will be forgiven' (5:15)?

We have already seen that James sets the elders' ministry in the context of a mutual recognition of faults. But is he now giving a blanket guarantee of a physical cure?

The words 'save' and 'raise him up' seem ambiguous. We want to ask James: 'Do you mean *physical* cure, or *final* cure?' Perhaps his answer would be 'Yes'! For God has given a specific universally applicable promise that we can claim for each sick person: 'everyone who calls on the name of the LORD shall be saved' (Joel 2:32, cited in Acts 2:21; Rom. 10:13). We are also given implicit general promises about God, that he has compassion on and heals the sick and broken-hearted and will raise up the needy (Psa. 113:7; 145:14). The 'prayer of faith' is interceding for others and making our requests to God based on such promises.

We therefore misunderstand James if we speak or act as though the origin of the power to raise up resides in the amount or degree of faith we exercise. No, it rests in God and in his word. And yet, on the other hand, God's word of promise summons us to 'act faith' (as older writers used to express it).

James is not giving us a slot-machine formula: 'Put in faith, and out will come healing. If not, it is because you have not put in enough faith.' The key lies in the promises of God. Mustard seed size faith is all that is needed (Matt. 17:20). For the power of answered prayer lies in God himself, in his character and in his promises. That is what a righteous (= faithful to the covenant) person recognizes.

So, here is a regular ministry of the elders that anyone who is sick may request. It is also a spiritual ministry and involves us in acknowledging not only our needs but also our sins. It is a prayer ministry, and it is also a faith ministry in which our elders are to spread before God all that he has revealed about himself in his word, and in which they claim the specific promises he has given to his people.

Could it be that, sometimes, we do not have because we do not ask (4:2)? Do we believe that God 'is able to do far more abundantly than all we ask or think' (Eph. 3:20)? This is then a ministry that contains a deep challenge both for elders and for anyone who is sick.

James has now addressed three 'categories' of people in the congregation: anyone who is (i) suffering, or (ii) cheerful, or (iii) sick. He now turns to a final group: those who are—

WANDERING

In addressing each of these four categories of readers ('Is anyone … Is anyone … Is anyone … if anyone', 5:13, 14, 19), James indicates where the responsibility lies. It is the responsibility of those who are suffering and the cheerful to pray or praise. Those who are sick have a responsibility to call for the elders who in turn have a responsibility to pray over them, anointing them; in doing so there is a mutual responsibility to confess our sins to one another.

But notice where the responsibility lies in the fourth category, when 'anyone among you wanders from the truth' (5:19). Here the exhortation is addressed to the entire church family ('My brothers', 5:19). Once again James's emotions seem to be heightened. He appeals to his readers as 'My brothers' (cf. 5:7, 12). He is concerned now about 'anyone' who 'wanders from the truth'. He had earlier used this verb ('wanders'—it is the root of our word 'planet') in chapter 1:16 of being deceived.

The kind of backsliding which leads to full apostasy from Christ does not happen in a single moment.

Think here of Judas Iscariot, whose departure from Christ is gradually traced in the Gospels. At first, he was only tempted to steal from the finances of the little apostolic band in which he served as treasurer (John 12:4-6); but then he transferred more fully to 'the dark side' (13:2), until eventually Satan inhabited his soul (13:27). Ananias and Sapphira sought only a better reputation than their lives merited, but it led them to place their feet on the pathway to death (Acts 5:1-10). Demas simply began to lose his love for the appearing of Christ as it was gradually edged out by a love for this world (2 Tim. 4:8b, 10). These examples give force to the exhortation in Hebrews that 'we must pay much closer attention to what we have heard, lest we drift away from it' (Heb. 2:1). Drifting is easy. We need to keep our eyes fixed on Christ.

But what is to be done when someone in the church family begins to drift? Especially in the light of what James has said to those who are sick ('call for the elders'), we ought to notice the difference in the exhortation here. It is not addressed to the wanderer (he is not listening). But neither is it addressed exclusively to the elders! How easy to say (and how often it is said!): 'the elders should do something about him ...' or 'the pastors should do something ... she's backsliding'. But this is to limit the responsibilities of family life to its leadership. The New Testament emphasizes, in contrast, that the ministry of the word in the church is intended to lead all members of the church family to sense their responsibility to each other. For our ascended Lord has given 'pastors and teachers ...' so that, 'speaking the truth in love, we are to grow up in every way into him who is the head, into Christ, from whom the whole body, joined and held together by every joint with which it is equipped, *when each part is working properly*, makes the body grow so that it builds itself up in love' (Eph. 4:15-16).

Remember Jesus' 'somebody-should-do-something' parable of the Good Samaritan (Luke 10:25-37). Presumably both the priest and the Levite saw the injured man on the Jericho Road. But they kept on their journey, perhaps saying to themselves, 'Somebody should do something about him', and adding under their breath, 'but I have more important things to do', or perhaps, 'I don't have the time just now ...' or even 'I don't have the skills this man needs in his state ... If I did have them, of course I would go over to help him ....' If someone in the church family wanders from the truth we all have a responsibility. It does not matter exactly who brings him back. What does matter is that there is someone who brings him back! We should not misapply these words to mean 'someone else, but not I'. Rather, when we sense this is happening to anyone in our church family we should begin to pray for them, where possible spend time with them, care for them, and yes, enlist others to do the same. It takes courage; it can be very costly. And in addition, it needs to be done both spiritually and gently (see Gal. 6:1).

James concludes not only this section but his entire letter by reminding us of both the motivation and the privilege involved in restoring the wanderer.

We need to know that 'whoever brings back a sinner from his wandering will save his soul from death and will cover a multitude of sins' (James 5:20). These words contain an allusion to Ezekiel 3:16–27 in which God set Ezekiel as a watchman for the house of Israel, giving him the solemn responsibility of seeking to bring others to repentance. That is accomplished when the person is brought back to Christ whose atoning blood covers all our sins (Rom. 3:23-25).

We believe in the priesthood of all believers. But we also—in this sense at least—believe in the prophethood of all believers too. For there is a 'whoever' in relation to restoring the wanderer just as much as there was a 'whoever' in relation to our coming to Christ in the first place (cf. John 3:16). And what a privilege it is to be that *whoever* who brings back a sinner from his wandering. It means nothing less than 'saving his soul from death'.

All through this letter James has been testing our faith. So much of what he wrote poses the same questions:

What kind of believer am I? Am I real?

What kind of fellowship are we? Do we care about the eternal salvation of others?

Those are the issues we need to settle before we lay this powerful letter aside.

Group Study Guide

SCHEME FOR GROUP BIBLE STUDY
(Covers 13 weeks; before each study read the passage indicated and the chapters from this book listed below)

STUDY PASSAGE		CHAPTERS
1.	James 1:1-4	Introduction and 1
2.	James 1:5-11	2
3.	James 1:12-18	3
4.	James 1:19-27	4
5.	James 2:1-13	5
6.	James 2:14-26	6
7.	James 3:1-12	7
8.	James 3:13-18	8
9.	James 4:1-6	9
10.	James 4:7-12	10
11.	James 4:13–5:6	11–12
12.	James 5:7-12	13
13.	James 5:13-20	14

This Study Guide has been prepared for group Bible study, but it can also be used individually. Those who use it on their own may find it helpful to keep a note of their responses in a notebook.

The way in which group Bible studies are led can greatly enhance their value. A well-conducted study will appear as though it has been easy to lead, but that is usually because the leader has worked hard and planned well. Clear aims are essential.

AIMS

In all Bible study, individual or corporate, we have several aims:

1. To gain an understanding of the original meaning of the particular passage of Scripture;

2. To apply this to ourselves and our own situation;

3. To develop some specific ways of putting the biblical teaching into practice.

2 Timothy 3:16-17 provides a helpful structure. Paul says that Scripture is useful for:

(i)   teaching us;

(ii)   rebuking us;

(iii)   correcting, or changing us;

(iv)   training us in righteousness.

Consequently, in studying any passage of Scripture, we should always have in mind these questions:

What does this passage teach us (about God, ourselves, etc.)?

Does it rebuke us in some way?

How can its teaching transform us?

What equipment does it give us for serving Christ?

In fact, these four questions alone would provide a safe guide in any Bible study.

PRINCIPLES

In group Bible study we meet in order to learn about God's Word and ways 'with all the saints' (Eph. 3:18). But our own experience, as well as Scripture, tells us that the saints are not always what they are called to be in every situation—including group Bible study! Leaders ordinarily have to work hard and prepare well if the work of the group is to be spiritually profitable. The following guidelines for leaders may help to make this a reality.

Preparation:

1. Study and understand the passage yourself. The better prepared and more sure of the direction of the study you are, the

more likely it is that the group will have a beneficial and enjoyable study. Ask: What are the main things this passage is saying? How can this be made clear? This is not the same question as the more common 'What does this passage "say to you"?', which expects a reaction rather than an exposition of the passage. Be clear about that distinction yourself, and work at making it clear in the group study.

2. On the basis of your own study form a clear idea *before* the group meets of (i) the main theme(s) of the passage which should be opened out for discussion, and (ii) some general conclusions the group ought to reach as a result of the study. Here the questions which arise from 2 Timothy 3:16-17 should act as our guide.

3. The guidelines and questions which follow may help to provide a general framework for each discussion; leaders should use them as starting places which can be further developed. It is usually helpful to have a specific goal or theme in mind for group discussion, and one is suggested for each study. But even more important than tracing a single theme is understanding the teaching and the implications of the passage.

Leading the Group:

1. Announce the passage and theme for the study, and begin with prayer. In group studies it may be helpful to invite a different person to lead in prayer each time you meet.

2. Introduce the passage and theme, briefly reminding people of its outline and highlighting the content of each subsidiary section.

3. Lead the group through the discussion questions. Use your own if you are comfortable in doing so; those provided may be used, developing them with your own points. As discussion proceeds, continue to encourage the group first of all to discuss the significance of the passage (teaching) and only then its application (meaning for us). It may be helpful to write important points and applications on a board by way of summary as well as visual aid.

4. At the end of each meeting, remind members of the group of their assignments for the next meeting, and encourage them to come prepared. Be sufficiently prepared as the leader to give specific assignments to individuals, or even couples or groups, to come with specific contributions.

5. Remember that you are the leader of the group! Encourage clear contributions, and do not be embarrassed to ask someone to explain what they have said more fully or to help them to do so ('Do you mean … ?').

Most groups include the 'over-talkative', the 'over-silent' and the 'red-herring raisers'! Leaders must control the first, encourage the second and redirect the third! Each leader will develop his or her own most natural way of doing that; but it will be helpful to think out what that is before the occasion arises! The first two groups can be helped by some judicious direction of questions to specific individuals or even groups (for example, 'Jane, you know something about this from personal experience …'); the third by redirecting the discussion to the passage itself ('That is an interesting point, but isn't it true that this passage really concentrates on … ?'). It may be helpful to break the group up into smaller groups sometimes, giving each subgroup specific points to discuss and to report back on. A wise arranging of these smaller groups may also help each member to participate.

More important than any techniques we may develop is the help of the Spirit enabling us to understand and to apply the Scriptures. Have and encourage a humble, prayerful spirit.

6. Keep faith with the schedule; it is better that some of the group wished the study could have been longer than that others are inconvenienced by it stretching beyond the time limits set.

7. Close in prayer. As time permits, spend the closing minutes in corporate prayer, encouraging the group to apply what they have learned in praise and thanks, intercession and petition.

Group Study Guide

STUDY 1: James 1:1-4

Introduction and Chapter 1

AIM: To understand the Christian's relationship to Jesus Christ as his 'servant' and to learn how to respond to trials in the Christian life.

1. As you read through James and study this letter, have in mind this question: How much of this teaching is an echo of what Jesus taught?

2. The idea that as Christians we are servants or slaves of Christ is common in the New Testament. Look up some other references where this description appears. What can you learn about your own Christian life from them? Or is this simply an outmoded term, if not a distasteful idea to us today?

3. What is to be the Christian's attitude to trials? How does James help us to develop it?

4. What would you say to a young Christian going through difficult experiences who asks you the question 'But how can I count this joy?'

5. Think of examples of steadfastness in Scripture and in people you know or about whom you have read. What can we learn from them?

STUDY 2: James 1:5-11

Chapter 2

AIM: To understand the nature and importance of wisdom in the Christian life.

1. How important is wisdom in Scripture?

2. In asking God to give us wisdom, and knowing that he does this through teaching us to apply Scripture and its principles to our lives, what passages in the Bible do you find particularly helpful?

3. What are some examples of being double-minded? What remedies can be applied?

4. What does it mean that a 'lowly brother' can 'boast in his exaltation'?

5. How can we live with a greater consciousness of the brevity of life?

STUDY 3: James 1:12-18

Chapter 3

AIM: To understand how temptation works and to learn how to resist it.

1. Are there ways in which Christians can blame God instead of taking personal responsibility in their lives?

2. What other examples of the 'temptation cycle' are there in Scripture, and how can we learn from them?

3. What do we need to learn in order to be aware of when and how we will be tempted?

4. Is it true that 'the seeds of every sin' are in each of our hearts, as Robert Murray M'Cheyne once wrote about himself? How is it that we seem to be tempted to different specific sins?

5. How can we be confident that God is good?

STUDY 4: James 1:19-27

Chapter 4

AIM: To learn how the Christian should use the tongue.

1. Is there a balance to be struck between speaking and not speaking, and if so how do we learn it?

2. In what ways are Christians today most likely to be deceived?

3. How can we read and study the Bible so that we do not forget what we see there?

4. What is an unbridled tongue, and how serious is it?

5. How did Jesus use the gift of speech and how can we follow his example?

STUDY 5: James 2:1-13

Chapter 5

AIM: To see the danger of partiality in the church and to learn how to respond to it.

1. Do you see danger signs in your own life or in your church family of the sin that James describes here in verses 1 to 4?

2. What creates this tendency?

3. What can cure it?

4. Are Christians going to be judged? If so, on what basis? Do other passages of Scripture shed light on this? What effect should this have on our lives?

5. Are all transgressions of the commandments of God equal?

STUDY 6: James 2:14-26

Chapter 6

AIM: To understand the relationship between justification by grace and good works.

1. If James were writing to the church today, would he need to include this section?

2. How can we avoid the twin dangers of legalism on the one hand and indifference to good works on the other?

3. Reflect on and discuss the teaching James gives here in the light of Jesus' teaching in Matthew 5:14-16 and 7:24-27 and in other passages in the Gospels.

4. How would you express as simply as you can the relationship between faith and works?

5. Reflect on and discuss the following statement from *The Westminster Confession of Faith* XVI. 2:

> These good works, done in obedience to God's commandments, are the fruits and evidences of a true and lively faith: and by them believers manifest their thankfulness, strengthen their assurance, edify their brethren, adorn the profession of the gospel, stop the mouths of the adversaries, and glorify God, whose workmanship they are, created in Christ Jesus thereunto; that, having their fruit unto holiness, they may have the end, eternal life.

STUDY 7: James 3:1-12

Chapter 7

AIM: To appreciate that teaching God's word is a very serious task and responsibility, and to learn more about the control of the tongue.

1. If someone told you they wanted to teach God's word to others, what would you say to them based on this passage?

2. Why is it so difficult to control the tongue?

3. Is remaining silent the same thing as the mastery of the tongue?

4. What lines of practical help can you trace in this passage?

5. How does this passage teach us we should pray for those who have been appointed teachers in the church?

STUDY 8: James 3: 13-18

Chapter 8

AIM: To learn what practical wisdom is.

1. Look up the passages listed in the first paragraph of the exposition. What do they tell us about wisdom?

2. Is it important or helpful to understand the intellectual revolution that lies behind our culture today? Does growing in biblical wisdom also mean being able to 'see through' to what lies behind cultural changes?

3. What are some elements in the contemporary culture that you see being influenced by the fact that 'the world did not know God through wisdom' (1 Cor. 1:21). In what ways do you see the exchange of wisdom for folly (Romans 1:21-32) being worked out in our society today? How should the Christian respond?

4. Describe a wise person in terms of James's teaching in this passage. What biblical characters were wise? Do you know someone who is wise? If so, what has made them wise?

5. What kind of person does Scripture see as foolish?

STUDY 9: James 4:1-6

Chapter 9

AIM: To understand what lies behind divisions in the church and to study the lifestyle that will prevent them.

1. Describe a quarrel you have witnessed in your own church or heard about in another church, and the explanations that have been given for it. What is the explanation James gives? Does his explanation shed light on the quarrels you have seen?

2. In what ways are we in danger of making friends of the world today?

3. How important is it to you that God is a jealous God? Does it make any impact on and difference to your Christian life? If it does, what is that impact? If not, why not?

4. In what ways do we see God opposing the proud (a) in Scripture and (b) in life?

5. Can you think of people in the Bible who submitted to God and were given grace?

STUDY 10: James 4:7-12

Chapter 10

AIM: To understand and apply the series of practical exhortations James gives.

1. This is the only place James mentions the devil. Is there a reason he refers to him here?

2. James tells us to resist the devil; but how are we to do that?

3. The language James uses in verses 8b to 10 is very dramatic. Is he simply using hyperbole? What do you think his words are meant to teach us?

4. We all know that humility is a prized virtue in the Bible; but how do we humble ourselves?

5. Do you ever hear evil spoken against a fellow Christian? How should we react and respond when a fellow Christian's name is mentioned, and the first words people speak about him are critical and harsh?

STUDY 11: James 4:13–5:6

Chapters 11–12

AIM: To take to heart the warnings James gives about a wrong focus in our lives or a sinful attitude to others.

1. Do modern Christians think much about the uncertainty of life and its brevity? How can we do this without feeling paralyzed?

2. How can we make either personal plans or business plans without being presumptuous?

3. What principles should govern the Christian's attitude to wealth?

4. Does it make any difference to the way we think about and live our lives that we are living in 'the last days'?

5. Are there any ways in which we fall under the condemnation of James 5:4?

STUDY 12: James 5:7-12

Chapter 13

AIM: To learn how to live the Christian life in the light of Christ's future coming and to live in his providences in the light of his purposes in our lives.

1. How often do you reflect on 'the coming of the Lord'? How important a role does it play in the teaching of the New Testament on Christian living?

2. In what sense is the Lord 'at hand'?

3. What other passages in Scripture speak about 'grumbling' among God's people? How is it addressed? What should we do about it if we notice it in (a) ourselves or (b) our church family?

4. From your knowledge of the story of Job, how do you think he remained steadfast?

5. What does it mean in today's world to let your 'yes' be yes and your 'no' be no?

STUDY 13: James 5:13-20

Chapter 14

AIM: To learn how to respond to the variety of experiences we have as individual Christians or in the fellowship of the church family.

1. We are told to pray when we are suffering. But what should we pray?

2. When we are cheerful, what should we sing?

3. When someone in our church family is sick today, is it important that we follow the pattern James describes?

4. Are there some guidelines you could formulate for how best to 'confess your sins to one another and pray for one another'?

5. Discuss the nature of the prayer of faith and how James's teaching here affects how we pray.

6. When someone 'wanders from the truth' and we are called to restore them, how can we avoid either (a) ignoring or (b) being overbearing in the way we handle the situation?

FOR FURTHER READING

The following books are recommended for further study of James:

JOHN BLANCHARD, *Truth For Life*, Darlington: Evangelical Press, 1986.

DAN G. MCCARTNEY, *James* (*Baker Exegetical Commentary on the New Testament*), Grand Rapids: Baker Academic, 2009.

THOMAS MANTON, *The Epistle of James* (*Geneva Series of Commentaries*), Edinburgh: Banner of Truth Trust, 1998.

CHRISTOPHER W. MORGAN, *A Theology of James* (*Explorations in Biblical Theology*), Phillipsburg, N.J.: P&R Publishing, 2010.

J. A. MOTYER, *The Message of James* (*The Bible Speaks Today*), Leicester: IVP, 1985.